THE WORST CALL EVER!

The Most Infamous Calls Ever Blown by Referees, Umpires, and Other Blind Officials

KYLE GARLETT & PATRICK O'NEAL

Collins

An Imprint of HarperCollinsPublishers

HarperCollins books may be purchased for educational, business, or sales promotional use. For information please write: Special Markets Department, HarperCollins Publishers, 10 East 53rd Street, New York, NY 10022.

First Collins paperback edition published 2008

Designed by Renato Stanisic

Library of Congress Cataloging-in-Publication Data is available upon request.

ISBN: 978-0-06-125137-5 (pbk.)

08 09 10 11 12   ID/RRD   10 9 8 7 6 5 4 3 2 1

CONTENTS

FOREWORD

Hmmmm . . . I bet you're wondering why I was asked to write the foreword. NO YOU'RE NOT!!! *The Worst Call Ever*—who else could be better qualified? The only thing I'm pissed off about is that Patrick and Kyle beat me to the punch. But since I've yet to miss a call my entire career (until now!) I would at least like to get my two cents in. As a matter of fact, I was recently playing a doubles event on the ATP (Association of Tennis Professionals) circuit when my doubles partner and I got screwed on a call on set point, and then . . . okay, don't get me started, that story may be in the second edition.

The point is that bad calls or a referee's poor decision can unfortunately alter the outcome of a match, game, or even championship. Now I'm pretty sure that no umpire wants to be the reason a game is lost (except in my case!), and even I know that their job is a pretty thankless task. I mean, I ask you, what type of person would want to be in a line of work where if they do a good job, they are not noticed? But hey, I never asked them to do it.

Anyway, when it comes to being passionate about sports officiating, I think I may have met my match in Patrick O'Neal.

Countless times over the years, Patrick and I have been glued to the TV set or at the event itself where I, of all people, would be telling him to calm down over what he considered to be a bad call. "You cannot be serious!" he'd shout, and I would immediately think to myself, *wait a minute, that's my line.* "Mac, the Lakers got screwed again! Come on man, did you see that call?" he'd say. We would be at a Rangers game at Madison Square Garden, and Patrick would blurt out, "That's the worst call ever!" Ironic, huh? Football on the boob tube also provided us with ample opportunities to dump on the officiating and vent our frustrations. When all was said and done, I long ago realized that Patrick belonged in the sports world because he was so passionate, opinionated, and obviously loved it so much. I'm happy that he has found his niche.

Kyle Garlett has done a nice job researching, reviewing, and reviving old arguments and memories that are etched in many athletes' minds, and ones that have certainly been heatedly debated by countless fans over generations. This book will undoubtedly spark new debates, and revisit some old wounds. A lot of the calls Patrick and Kyle write about are subjective, and can certainly be argued one way or another. I know this is hard to believe, but I don't agree with all of them. Did Michael push off? Did Brady fumble? Did McEnroe get the shaft? (Yes, yes, and most definitely yes!) The point is that it's healthy to have a good debate every now and then, and even a good old-fashioned argument. I think Patrick and Kyle have tapped into something with *The Worst Call Ever.* I hope you feel the same way.

—**John McEnroe**

Mother, may I slug the umpire
May I slug him right away?
So he cannot be here, Mother
When the clubs begin to play?
Let me clasp his throat, dear mother
In a dear, delightful grip
With one hand, and with the other
Bat him several in the lip.
Let me climb his frame, dear mother
While the happy people shout;
I'll not kill him, dearest mother
I will only knock him out.
Let me mop the ground up, Mother,
With this person, dearest do;
If the ground can stand it, Mother
I don't see why you can't, too.
Mother, may I slug the umpire
Slug him right between the eyes?
If you let me do it, Mother
You shall have the champion prize.
—ANONYMOUS, PUBLISHED IN
The Chicago Tribune (1886)

INTRODUCTION

One night when longtime American League umpire Ron Luciano was working a minor league game in Pittsfield, Massachusetts, the pregame preparations were set to conclude, as they always did, with the nightly playing of "The Star-Spangled Banner." But as the often-used and badly scratched recording began to play on the stadium's sound system, its old turntable couldn't get the vinyl record past the first scratch.

The familiar ballgame prelude began, "Oh, say can you see . . ." then "Oh, say can you see . . ." and again "Oh, say can you see . . ."

After four or five repetitions of the Anthem's opening line, an opportunistic and quick-witted fan in the stands shouted at Luciano, "I guess they know who's umpiring tonight!"

Such is the disrespect that follows all of the men and women charged with keeping our sporting events fair. It is a thankless job that requires a thick skin and a short memory. They are routinely abused, ridiculed, and vilified. And even when they do their job well—which is the vast majority of the time—one or two lone mistakes out of a thousand right calls counters their competence.

Whether they're wearing umpire blue, a referee's black and white, or one of the rainbow of colors that soccer referees must have in their closets, when each of them takes the field, court, ice, ring, or pitch, they do so with a bright-red bull's-eye on their back that attracts acrimony like a giant magnet for malevolence. The unavoidable reality is, you could put Stephen Hawking in a striped shirt and hand him a whistle, and there will be some group of otherwise intelligent and clearheaded fans who would think him a simpleminded idiot.

As keepers of truth and enlightenment, we point out the inherently unjust world that referees and umpires find themselves living in to help temper what we have sought to do through writing this book: expose their most injurious mistakes, document their lasting damage—which to some wronged parties has evolved into a condition akin to post-traumatic stress disorder—and perhaps, with enough elucidation, spread the soothing balm of reconciliation.

Although, if all of that sounds like too grandiose a goal, we'll settle for exposition.

Our first task was to determine which sports grievances deserved inclusion in our final tally of events. Not all thievery is created equal.

October doesn't own the market on bad baseball calls. But for our purposes, a missed third strike that sent the 1997 Pirates to a fourth straight loss in May doesn't make the cut. Nor does a November basketball game decided by a questionable charging call, a missed pass interference that determined fourth place in the Sun Belt Conference, or an uncalled double-fault at the Zagreb Indoors that kept Flavio Cipolla from cracking the ATP's top-150.

If it was big, memorable, ridiculous, rule-changing, particularly egregious, decidedly dishonest, or ultimately championship-deciding, you'll find it here.

Also, anguish at the hands of offending officials is definitely in the eye of the season-ticket beholder. The improbable "Music City Miracle"—the play that sent the Bills to a playoff defeat in Nashville on January 8, 2000—brings Buffalonians to tears faster than the hottest of chicken wings. But sorry, Bills fans, your pain is not our pursuit. The unbiased eye not clouded by the skies of Western New York can see that Frank Wycheck's lateral to Kevin Dyson was indeed just that, a lateral ("to pass the ball sideways or backward"). The play was legal and called correctly, and an unforgettable NFL moment for everyone who watched it.

Furthermore, it has been suggested (by Knicks fans) that Reggie Miller's career-defining eight points in less than nine seconds to win a 1995 playoff game in New York be included because during the sequence he allegedly shoved Greg Anthony to steal the inbounds pass that set up his second consecutive 3-pointer. No dice, New Yorkers. We advocate less referee interference at the end of games, not more. And seriously, even Spike Lee is a balanced-enough fan to give Miller credit for one of the great postseason moments in NBA history, while placing the blame for the shame on the five Knicks standing catatonically on the Madison Square Garden floor.

This is not to say that we eliminated all controversy from our list, or even shied away from it. The infamous "tuck rule" that took down the Raiders in a playoff game at New England in 2002 was technically applied correctly by the game's officials, and the NFL to this day defends the call as it stood that snowy evening. But for us, it's front and center in our NFL section. The correct application of this rule defies all logic, and the resulting ramifications of the confusing call are simply too big for us to ignore.

We have also included Lance Armstrong's much-debated run

at the Tour de France for the very specific reason that it's created such controversy. The Tour's rules on drug testing, mirroring many other international sports, are very specific on what concludes a positive test for a banned substance. The complexities of testing human blood, and the many exterior factors that can affect the test, demand checks and balances. Yet despite the fact that Armstrong has never crossed the positive-test threshold, the officials of the race have labeled him a cheat.

Obviously many sports fans, athletes, coaches, writers, and officials will disagree with some of our selections, while questioning our exclusion of others. But that's what we love so much about sports—the endless debate that fills sports bars and divides opinion along team-loyalty lines. It's a place where right and wrong is defined almost exclusively by which parties are doing the disagreeing.

And since what we also love about debating sports is the incessant number of top-10 lists that the back-and-forth bickering is prone to spawn (a personal favorite is "top-10 ballpark hot dogs"), we present our scientifically determined top-10 "Worst Calls Ever."

#10 Pine Tar (p. 21) Okay, so right out of the gate we have violated our rule about regular-season baseball. The "pine tar" game and incident happened in July. But it didn't officially end until August, and any baseball game that takes three weeks to finish because of an umpire's call has to be included.

#9 The Tuck Rule (p. 87) Using their rulebook, the NFL makes a compelling argument in favor of the way the referees ruled on Tom Brady's fumble in 2002. The problem is that the visual evidence makes the league sound like a pack of fools. If it looks like a fumble, walks like a fumble, and quacks like a fumble, in our book it's a fumble.

#8 **Boston Garden Sun Set** (p. 49) It happened pre-Magic Johnson and Larry Bird, so it's possible the Game 5 gem of the 1976 NBA Finals has failed to register on many an NBA fan's permanent radar. But for the Phoenix Suns, the arrogance that robbed them of a potential world title is an unforgettable moment of injustice.

#7 **Jobbed, Pound-for-Pound** (p. 171) Boxer Roy Jones Jr. wasn't the victim of arrogance or misjudgment at the 1988 Seoul Summer Olympics. His gold medal ring dreams were destroyed by a collection of criminal acts.

#6 **The Legend of Jeffrey Maier** (p. 12) We all saw the helping hand of the twelve-year-old Yankee fan reach over the right-field wall to assist Derek Jeter's pivotal 1996 ALCS home run in Game 1. So why didn't umpire Rich Garcia?

#5 **Creased Cup** (p. 76) The Dallas Stars and Buffalo Sabres. Triple overtime in Game 6 of the Stanley Cup Finals. Dominik Hasek and Brett Hull. Skate, puck, crease, and goal. Enough said.

#4 **Hand of God** (p. 201) The world's biggest stage is the quadrennial World Cup. And its biggest star in 1986, other than Argentina's Diego Maradona, was the big man himself, God.

#3 **Don Denkinger's Show-Me State Shame** (p. 4) It is the most famous blown call in baseball history, turning what was otherwise a mundane World Series beyond the borders of Missouri into an enduring Fall Classic controversy that handed Kansas City its one and only championship.

#2 **Cold War Compromised** (p. 167) You'll be hard pressed to find many more outrageous injustices than the scurrilous events that led to Soviet Union gold at the 1972 Olympics men's basketball tournament. We could find only one.

#1 Fifth Down (p. 132) Why do we give the nod to Colorado's fifth-down win at Missouri in 1990 over the 1972 Olympic basketball finals? Because seven professional (allegedly) officials—grown men with educations, jobs, and presumably brains—failed to correctly count to *four*. Their simultaneous regression into enumeration imbecility handed Colorado the game and eventually the National Championship.

As you read through the ninety-four plays and events of malfeasance that were ferreted out and featured in this book, and while formulating your own top-10 list of worst calls (because it's what sports fans do), you can choose to heed the impassioned plea of Ian "Scotty" Morrison, the former NHL referee-in-chief:

> Boo the players, but leave the referees alone. They're doing a difficult job well and they don't need 5,000 assistants.

Or you can ignore him, and boo away, exercising with pride the right that every fan has enjoyed since a poorly sighted caveman first grabbed a whistle, donned black and white stripes, and started officiating disputed clubbing competitions.

An umpire who claims he never missed a play is . . . well, an umpire.
—RON LUCIANO
AMERICAN LEAGUE UMPIRE (1968–1980)

It's wonderful to be here, to be able to hear the baseball against the bat, ball against the glove, and to be able to boo the umpire.
—GENERAL DOUGLAS MACARTHUR
AT A BASEBALL GAME AFTER WORLD WAR II

I never questioned the integrity of an umpire. Their eyesight, yes.
—LEO DUROCHER
HALL OF FAME PLAYER/MANAGER

MAJOR LEAGUE BASEBALL

Whether baseball's origins date back to the fourteenth-century English game of stoolball—where a batter stood before an upturned three-legged stool while another player pitched a ball to him—or is the younger brother of the old Russian game lapta—as is claimed by several old Soviet Union-era encyclopedias—or was invented in 1839 by future West Point graduate Abner Doubleday—even though he never actually made such a claim—today a trip to the ballpark is as decidedly American as mom, apple pie, and reality television.

For an idea on just how popular baseball is in America, look no further than Hollywood, the land of the coveted superfluous buck. Scores of baseball films have been turned out by Hollywood's entertainment conveyor belt of slop: from the *Bad News Bears* trilogy, only slightly less impressive than Peter Jackson's *Lord of the Rings*, to *Ed*, the exception that proves the rule that everyone loves a monkey, to *Hardball* starring Keanu Reeves (see *Ed*).

As a nation, the sport has so engrained itself into the fabric of our society that its language has become a significant piece of our own. We've all, at one time, been motivated to *step up to the plate* by someone playing *hardball*, even if they were coming *out of left field*. And whether or not you were *swinging for the fences* or just *covering all your bases*, this is *the big leagues*, and hopefully you didn't *drop the ball*.

But when it comes to an afternoon at the ballpark, no fan wants to get bogged down in an analysis of the etymological relationship between our national pastime and the more than 600,000 words that are found in the *Oxford English Dictionary*. For them, baseball is about peanuts, red hots, and 10-cent beer night—and of course, every fan's God-given right to curse the men in blue.

> *Any umpire's decision which involves judgment, such as, but not limited to, whether a batted ball is fair or foul, whether a pitch is a strike or a ball, or whether a runner is safe or out, is final. No player, manager, coach or substitute shall object to any such judgment decisions.*
> —Rule 9.02(a) Official Rules of Major League Baseball

Don Denkinger's Show-Me State Shame
October 26, 1985: World Series Game 6, Cardinals at Royals

The most widely circulated legend as to the origins of the appellation "Show-Me State" attributes the phrase to an 1899 speech given by Missouri congressman Willard Duncan Vandiver. While at a banquet in Philadelphia, Vandiver declared, "I come from a state that raises corn and cotton and cockleburs, and frothy eloquence neither convinces nor satisfies me. I am from Missouri. You have got to show me."

It is assumed that the "show me" moniker stuck after scores of puzzled but curious East Coast banquetgoers asked Vandiver if he could show them what a cocklebur was.

And ironically, after the Show-Me State World Series eighty-

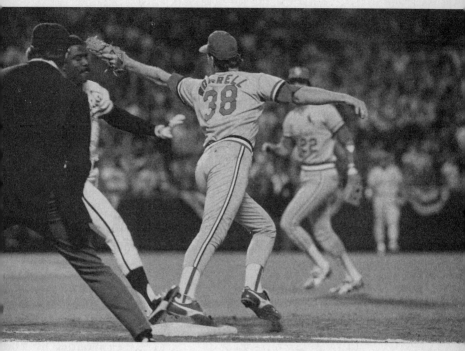

Game 6, 1985 World Series: Umpire Don Denkinger takes his fateful dive into Fall Classic infamy.

six years later, the word *cocklebur* (or one of its more adult variations) was used by St. Louis Cardinals fans to describe American League umpire Don Denkinger.

Following an improbable NLCS victory over the Dodgers, where Ozzie Smith won Game 5 with his first ever left-handed home run, and Jack Clark won the deciding Game 6 with a 3-run homer in the ninth—both coming off Tom Niedenfuer for you scoring at home—the Cardinals went into the 1985 World Series against the Royals as heavy favorites to win.

And after Kansas City dropped the series' first two games at home (no team in World Series history had ever rallied from such a fate to take the title), it was a foregone conclusion that St. Louis would be raising its tenth championship banner. In fact, it was a surprise to most that the Cardinals failed to close the door at Busch Stadium—dropping two of three games—and were forced to go back to Kansas City to finally pop their champagne.

But the moment for bubbly was finally at hand in Game 6, as the Cardinals entered the bottom of the ninth inning up 1-0 and a perfect 88-0 on the season when leading after eight innings. Rookie closer Todd Worrell, who struck out a World Series record-tying six consecutive Royals in Game 5, was on the mound to nail it down. And just three outs separated St. Louis from their second World Championship in four years, and the I-70 Series win.

Just three outs—and first base umpire Don Denkinger.

Pinch hitter Jorge Orta led off the inning with an innocent ground ball to first baseman Jack Clark, who then flipped the ball to the covering Worrell, who beat Orta to the bag by a full step—as seen by everyone in the stadium but the one and only man who really mattered, Don Denkinger.

His call was "safe," and despite a series of rapid-fire reenactments by Worrell, protests from Clark, and what looked to be a steady stream of obscenities from manager Whitey Herzog, Denkinger didn't budge.

The next batter, Steve Balboni, popped up along the first base dugout—only to be given new life when the still-fuming Clark misplayed the ball. Balboni then got a single, and a pinch runner, a bunt out, and a passed ball later, the Royals had runners at second and third and a chance to win with Dane Iorg at the plate.

Iorg, who hit .529 in the Cardinals' 1982 World Series win, came up clutch for K.C., lining a single to right field that chased home Onix Concepcion and Jim Sundberg for the 2-1 comeback victory.

The following day in Game 7, with Denkinger now behind home plate, the demoralized Cardinals disgraced their way to an 11-0 loss, handing Kansas City its first and only World Series crown.

It'd be easy to point to World Series MVP Bret Saberhagen's two complete games and 0.50 ERA as the reason for the Royals' win. Or the Cardinals' .185 series batting average and just two stolen bases, following a regular season where they led the National League in both categories at .264 and 314 respectively.

But as any baseball fan living in the St. Louis metropolitan area, and quite a few other places, will tell you, Don Denkinger deserves all the credit/blame.

Banished to the Bookies
June 24, 1882: National League

Attorney William R. Wheaton became the first officially recorded baseball umpire on October 6, 1845, as directed by the Knickerbocker Club of New York, which is largely credited with transforming the game into its "modern" version. According to its rules, the club's president "shall appoint an Umpire, who shall keep the game in a book provided for that purpose, and note all violations of the Bylaws and Rules."

The rules governing who exactly was qualified to umpire a baseball game, however, were far from exact.

Two umpires, one chosen by each team, was the common practice in the 1850s. Which naturally resulted in more than a few conflicting rulings. Later a single umpire—usually a spectator or player chosen by the home team, but sanctioned by the visiting captain—became the norm. But that, of course, made consistency from game to game next to impossible.

Finally in 1879, a year after the National League instructed the home teams to pay the umpires $5 a game (previously they were volunteers only), league president William A. Hulbert appointed the first-ever umpire staff. It consisted of twenty men designated as "fit" to be umpires, living in or near cities where the league had teams. That meant that an umpire would always work games for his hometown team, which of course led to more than one case of "homering"—the act of making calls based on the proximity of your home to those of the fans that you've just enraged.

In the case of Richard Higham, a .300 hitting player/manager throughout the 1870s turned Detroit Wolverines umpire in 1881 and 1882—the opposite was true. It was at the expense of the home team that he makes our book.

In 1882 the value of an umpire's $5 a game paycheck was nothing to sneeze at. Its worth was almost equivalent today to $100 a game. And in the age of the owner's secret reserve clause plus a $2,500 salary cap imposed by owner and league strongman Albert Goodwill Spalding—because in his 1881 words, "professional baseball is on the wane . . . salaries must come down . . . bankruptcy stares every team in the face"—the umpires made a decent wage. And by written rule they were allowed to eject any spectator that "hisses or hoots." And what could possibly lead someone to jeopardize all of that? Simple: greed.

Higham determined that $5 a game was not nearly enough for his services. And using his unique position as the arbiter of all things Detroit baseball, the player and manager who had been dogged late in his career by rumors that his play hadn't always been on the level took an undeniable turn to the dark side. He began to collude with area gamblers.

In June of 1882, after a series of close calls went against his Wolverines, team president and mayor of Detroit William Thompson began to suspect that Higham had interests beyond fair baseball. Following his instincts, Thompson hired a private investigator, who turned up a series of coded telegrams that Higham had sent to a well-known gambler. The phrase "buy all the lumber you can" meant lay your money down on Detroit. No telegram meant no joy for the home team. Bet against them.

To be fair, there is one scholar with the Society of American Baseball Research who says Higham was never the subject of Thompson's suspicions or a private detective's investigation. And at no time was he confronted with evidence of any wrongdoing. Although it should also be noted that the dissenting opinion comes from Harold Higham, of the Richard Higham family.

What the rest of the research tells us, and what Major League Baseball considers the official version of events, is that when the National League was presented with the evidence gathered by Mayor Thompson's investigator, it fired Richard Higham on June 22. Then two days later on June 24, the league made Higham the first, and to this date only, umpire ever banned by baseball.

It was a hard lesson on the pitfalls of cavorting with gamblers that carried with it a stiff penalty, and one that has had to be learned over (Shoeless Joe Jackson) and over (Pete Rose) again.

Connie Mack's Malaise
September 30, 1907: Tigers at Athletics

In a little-known incident during the first game of a doubleheader between the New York Highlanders (they became the Yankees in 1913) and Connie Mack's Philadelphia Athletics on September 3, 1906, umpire Silk O'Loughlin, who would work the first of thirty-one career World Series games later that fall, was physically assaulted by the Highlanders' Kid Elberfeld to the point that police had to forcibly remove the shortstop from the field. New York won the game, 4-3.

In the second game, a disputed collision between New York's Willie Keeler and Philadelphia shortstop Lave Cross allowed two Highlander runners to come around and score. O'Loughlin, on edge and a little shell shocked from his earlier fight with

Elberfeld, ruled unequivocally that there was no interference on the play. And when Philadelphia captain Harry Davis got a little too animated during his argument over the questionable call, O'Loughlin declared the game a forfeit in New York's favor, handing them the doubleheader sweep.

Fast forwarding twelve months, once again the umpire was O'Loughlin, and he was again working an important late-season game involving Connie Mack's Philadelphia Athletics. This time the Detroit Tigers were in town for a critical series involving the American League's top two teams.

After a 5-4 Detroit win on Friday, a rainout on Saturday, and the mandatory day off on Sunday (can you imagine a time when Sunday was sports-free intentionally?), the A's and Tigers prepared to play two games on the final Monday of the regular season. For Philadelphia, the year would end that coming Saturday at the Washington Senators.

Game one of the twin bill was exactly what *The New York Times* had predicted it to be: "The greatest struggle in the history of baseball." With an overflow crowd packed to the rafters of Philadelphia's Columbia Park, and said to be fifteen fans deep along the outfield ropes, the A's jumped out to a hometown-delighting early 7-1 lead. But the Tigers battled back, and in the bottom of the ninth, trailing 8-6, future Hall of Famer Ty Cobb tied things up off future Hall of Fame pitcher Rube Waddell with a 2-run homer to right field.

After an uneventful 10th inning, a run across for each side in the 11th, and scoreless at bats in the 12th and 13th, the A's looked to have their chance to finally win it in the bottom of the 14th when Harry Davis (the same Harry Davis who'd argued with O'Loughlin causing a forfeit a year earlier) drove a fly ball into the crowd in left-center field that would ordinarily have been called a ground-rule double. But as Tigers centerfielder Sam Crawford ran over to the edge of the crowd, a policeman, who'd been sitting along the rope line on an overturned soda crate, stood up, prompting Detroit to cry foul and call for interference.

The A's contended that the officer was simply trying to get out of Crawford's way. And Mack alleged that O'Loughlin, who was umpiring behind the plate that day, acknowledged his agreement by remarking to on-deck batter Topsy Hartsel, "What are [the Tigers] arguing about? I saw no interference."

Base umpire Tommy Connolly claimed, however, that he did see the interference. And after the two umpires conferred for a few minutes—minutes filled with arguments in the stands and a fight on the field between the two teams (started by Cobb, of course)—O'Loughlin turned to Mack and the A's bench and called Davis out.

The already angry A's could barely contain their rage, exploding at O'Loughlin and accusing him of conspiracy beyond incompetence. Even the normally reserved Mack got into the heated argument, a vigorous protest that fell on deaf ears but managed to increase in intensity when the next batter up, Danny Murphy, stroked a single that would have easily sent Davis home with the winning run.

Instead, the two teams played three more scoreless innings before O'Loughlin ended the battle in a 9-9 tie and canceled the second game because of darkness. Unable to record the win they rightfully deserved, or get an opportunity to take the second half of the doubleheader, the Athletics finished the week, and the season, 1½ games behind the pennant-winning Tigers.

At the time of the dispute Mack told reporters, "If ever there was such a thing as crooked baseball, today's game would stand as a good example." Forty years later, nearing the end of a Hall of Fame career that resulted in five World Series titles and more than 3,700 wins, the "Grand Old Man of Baseball"—who sported his trademark fedora while managing for a Major League record 53 years—was still angry about 1907, recounting to reporters, "We could have won [the pennant] if Silk O'Loughlin hadn't called that decision against us."

The Legend of Jeffrey Maier
October 9, 1996: ALCS Game 1, Orioles at Yankees

At a certain level, the player-umpire relationship is always a bit frosty around the edges. But in October of 1996, things between the men who make up both sides of a Major League Baseball playing field were downright adversarial.

In the closing days of the regular season, and with the Baltimore Orioles in the heat of the playoff chase, Roberto Alomar protested a called third strike by spitting in the face of home plate umpire John Hirschbeck. Alomar then ratcheted up the outrage by claiming that Hirschbeck had been off his game and quick to anger ever since his eight-year-old son had died of the rare brain disease adrenoleukodystrophy (ALD) in 1993.

And just in case the umpires hadn't sufficiently circled the wagons in support of their comrade and against the all-star second baseman, the league office added their own insult by giving Alomar a five-game slap on the wrist suspension that he wouldn't have to serve until the following April. That soft ruling by American League President Gene Budig prompted the umpires' union to threaten a postseason walkout, which was only averted in the eleventh hour after an injunction filed by Major League Baseball was enforced by a federal judge the morning the playoffs were scheduled to begin.

So in the bottom of the eighth inning of Game 1 of the ALCS, and with the Orioles clinging to a 4-3 lead and a chance to steal the win at Yankee Stadium, no one should have been too surprised that things would end with the umpires again at the center of the firestorm, pitted against the O's.

Derek Jeter was at the plate, Armando Benitez was on the mound, and Tony Tarasco was in right field. But so were two other people: umpire Rich Garcia, a member of the umpires' executive board (coincidentally), and twelve-year-old Jeffrey Maier.

Game 1, 1996 ALCS: Jeffrey Maier becomes the most famous twelve-year-old baseball fan in America.

Jeter lofted a fly ball toward the short porch in right, but just as Tarasco was settling under it at the warning track to record the long out, the sixth-grade baseball fan reached out into the field of play—clearly interfering with Tarasco's ability to make the catch—and deflected the ball across the fence for a game-tying home run.

A frantic Oriole protest ensued, led by Tarasco and manager Davey Johnson. But Garcia, who had what appeared to be a clear view of the play, held fast to his home-run call. In his mind there was no fan interference. Although after the game, and after seeing the replays, Garcia did admit that he blew the call—an admission that might have won him some measure of absolution in Baltimore if he hadn't been seen in left field the following day signing autographs for grateful Yankee fans.

New York ended up winning Game 1 on an 11th-inning home run by Bernie Williams, eventually won the series in five games, and won the World Series, their first in eighteen years, over the Braves in six.

For twelve-year-old Jeffrey, the fame, which included an appearance on David Letterman, was fleeting. But the infamy has carried on. Jeffrey went to Wesleyan University in Middletown, Connecticut, to play baseball, where once as a sophomore (the year he was first-team all-conference) a game had to be stopped when fans at Williams College (Mass.) were pelting him with ice.

Hurled projectiles aside, Jeffrey actually has quite the sense of humor about his moment in the Major League spotlight. A student at Wesleyan made a film entitled *I Hate Jeffrey Maier*, about a guy from Baltimore who realizes he is classmates with Maier, and then devotes his college career to making Maier's life miserable.

Starring in the film and playing himself: Jeffrey Maier.

The Bambino, Bucky, Buckner, and Barnett
October 14, 1975: World Series Game 3, Red Sox at Reds

Finally, in 2004 the talismans, mystical stones, and sacrificed live chickens worked. The curse that defined a franchise for nearly a century was over.

Long-suffering Boston Red Sox fans can now forget about Johnny Pesky holding the cutoff throw, allowing Enos Slaughter's winning mad dash in 1946. They can once and for all forget that in 1948's one-game playoff loss to Cleveland, Sox manager Joe McCarthy sent Denny Galehouse to the mound while four better starters stayed seated in the dugout. And never again should a Sox fan denounce Bucky Dent (1978) or belittle Bill Buckner (1986).

And now, finally, Bostonians can stop recognizing 1918 as the origin of a curse, and instead celebrate it as the birth year of a legend: Ted Williams.

Of course that is now, and this was then, 1975, when the Curse of the Bambino was alive and well, and seemingly impervious.

Carlton Fisk's career-defining moment, and one of the all-time great moments in sports, would come in Game 6 of the '75 Series. How many times since then, from T-ball games to softball beer leagues, has a batter waived his home run fair? But that wasn't the only game of the series that Fisk had a hand in deciding. People often forget that it was his error in the tenth inning that cost the Sox a win in Game 3, although the blame for that blunder should fall squarely on the shoulders of home plate umpire Larry Barnett.

The Big Red Machine, on the back of home runs from Johnny Bench, Dave Concepcion, and Cesar Geronimo, raced out to an early 5-1 lead in Game 3. But a pinch-homer from Bernie Carbo in the seventh and a 2-run blast by Dwight Evans in the ninth brought the Sox back and sent the game to extra frames tied up 5-5.

The Red Sox went quietly in the top of the tenth. And in the bottom of the inning, ironically in this game that had seen six home runs, including a pair hit by future Hall of Famers, the loudest at bat of the night would send the ball about five feet off the bat of a career .245 hitter.

With Cesar Geronimo on first, reserve outfielder Ed Armbrister laid down a sacrifice bunt right in front of home plate. And then, hesitating as he left the batter's box, Armbrister got tangled up with Fisk, who was fielding the ball and attempting a throw to second to force out the lead runner.

Fisk's throw sailed high directly because of the interference.

And because home plate umpire Larry Barnett inexplicably failed to make the correct call (Armbrister should have been out on the spot, and Geronimo returned to first), Fisk's error sent Geronimo to third with the winning run. After an intentional walk to Pete Rose and a strikeout by Merv Rettenmund, Joe Morgan delivered the game-winning hit that put Cincinnati up 2 games to 1.

Everyone in attendance, and especially the two men broadcasting the game for NBC, Curt Gowdy and Tony Kubek, criticized the call as indefensible. And later, when Barnett began to receive death threats from outraged Red Sox fans, he specifically blamed Gowdy and Kubek for fanning the flames with their commentary.

On behalf of Barnett, Major League Baseball threatened to end its relationship with NBC if something wasn't done. That something turned out to be the firing of Gowdy, the man who had called the previous ten World Series and was later (1984) inducted into the broadcaster's wing of the Baseball Hall of Fame.

The next year Gowdy was replaced by Joe Garagiola, although NBC denied that Barnett's claims and Major League Baseball's anger had anything to do with the decision.

Madhouse at Home Plate
October 10, 1970: World Series Game 1, Orioles at Reds

The year 1975 was by no means the first time that Riverfront Stadium's home plate was the location for World Series controversy. Five years earlier, the multipurpose facility's dish had been christened as the place where umpires' reputations went to die, with Ken Burkhart being the original October sacrificial lamb.

You may know Game 1 of the 1970 World Series for Baltimore third baseman Brooks Robinson's incredible (and often replayed)

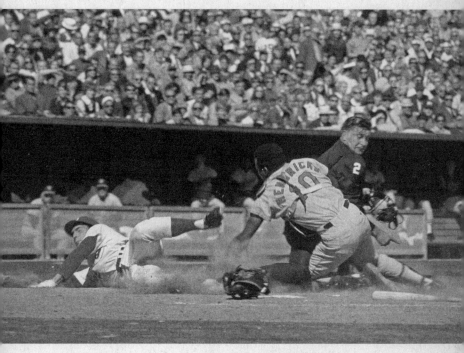

Game 1, 1970 World Series: Orioles catcher Elrod Hendricks, Reds runner Bernie Carbo, and umpire Ken Burkhart uncermoniously collide at home plate.

backhanded stab-and-throw-out of Cincinnati first baseman Lee May. But in that same sixth inning, when the fielding legend of a future Hall of Famer was born, so was a continuing Fall Classic controversy.

Following Robinson's circus play to record the first out in the bottom of the sixth, the Reds got their next two batters aboard, putting the lead run in a 3-3 game just ninety feet away for pinch hitter Ty Cline.

Cline, who would later call the at bat "my moment in the limelight," chopped Jim Palmer's big overhand curve into the dirt just in front of the plate. And as Orioles catcher Elrod Hendricks jumped up from his crouch to go out and field the ball, home plate umpire and crew chief Ken Burkhart followed him out to call it fair.

Burkhart's initial instincts were right. In anticipation of a play to first, he steered clear of Hendricks by straddling the third base line. And after grabbing the ball, Hendricks did turn to first base to throw out the sprinting Cline. But in a hurried change of heart, and much to Burkhart's dismay, Hendricks instead wheeled back toward the plate to go after the hard-charging lead runner, Bernie Carbo—and wheeled right into Burkhart.

Lunging for Carbo, and attempting to go through the umpire, Hendricks was able to apply the tag. And even though Burkhart had now become flattened roadkill along the third-base line, putting him in no position to see the play, the inordinately involved umpire signaled the runner out.

In his defense, Burkhart almost got it right. Hendricks's glove did beat Carbo to the plate. But what Burkhart failed to see from his unenviable position in the middle of the collision was that the glove was empty. The baseball was still firmly held in Hendricks's right throwing hand.

Not having seen the events that his high chopper put in motion, Cline asked Reds first-base coach Ted Kluzewski what happened. Big Klu pointed to the tangle of bodies, which now included crazed Reds manager Sparky Anderson, and said, "It's a madhouse at home plate."

The Orioles went on to win Game 1 by just 1 run; the next day Hendricks hit a game-winning 2-run double to put the O's up 2-0; and eventually Baltimore claimed the World Series crown in five games.

The always smiling Hendricks became a popular fixture behind the plate in Baltimore, in large part due to the theatrics and heroics that defined his 1970 World Series. And following his twelve-year playing career, he spent twenty-eight years with the organization as its bullpen coach—the longest coaching tenure in franchise history.

For Burkhart, a National League umpire for seventeen years, the 1970 World Series turned out to be his last.

Florida's Blue Plate Special
October 12, 1997: NLCS Game 5, Braves at Marlins

It was Roman philosopher Cicero who said, "It is fortune, not wisdom, that rules man's life." Well, consider the fortune that took twenty-two-year-old Cuban defector Livan Hernandez from a rookie pitcher cutting his teeth with a recent major league expansion team to being a household name.

In the 1997 NL Division Series against the Giants, Hernandez made a single four-inning relief appearance, but no starts. And he wasn't in manager Jim Leyland's rotation plans for the NLCS against the Braves. That was set up to be Kevin Brown (Games 1, 4, and 7), Alex Fernandez (Games 2 and 6), Tony Saunders (Game 3), and Al Leiter (Game 5).

But you know what Scottish poet Robert Burns penned: "The best laid plans of mice and men often go awry."

Things began to go awry the morning after Fernandez was beaten up in the Marlins' Game 2 loss. That's when doctors told the seventeen-game winner that he had a torn rotator cuff, and was done for the postseason. As it turned out, Fernandez never pitched another full season again, winning just eleven more games in his career.

So with Fernandez done, Hernandez now became the scheduled starter for Game 6. But with that still four days away, Leyland used him in relief in Game 3. No problem. He had plenty of time to rest.

But things continued to unravel the morning of Game 4. Kevin Brown was sick in bed with a viral infection, and had to be moved back in the rotation—twice: The first time swapping places with Al Leiter for a loss in Game 4, and the second time with Hernandez for Game 5—a rookie pitcher that hadn't completed a game all season, averaged less than six innings a start, and would now be taking the mound just two days after he'd pitched out of the pen.

Leyland, recognizing the dire straits his rotation was in, joked before the game, "I can't pull a rabbit out of a hat and put Sandy Koufax in a Marlins uniform. So we have to improvise. That's life."

In the first inning things started badly for Hernandez. Two batters in, and the Braves had runners at first and third with Chipper Jones at the plate. But that's when the biggest (in every sense of the word) participant of the evening, home plate umpire Eric Gregg, took center stage.

Hernandez got out of the jam by striking out in succession Jones, Fred McGriff, and Ryan Klesko. And after a Michael Tucker home run led off the second inning, Hernandez never allowed another runner past first base, striking out an NLCS record 15 Braves with the aid of an Eric Gregg strike zone that was only rivaled in size by his 300-plus-pound waistline. The final out of the Marlins 2-1 win came on a called strike three so far outside that it would have hit Fred McGriff if he'd been batting right-handed.

Later, Gregg would admit that he blew the call on McGriff's third and final strikeout of the game. But he continued to insist that the strike zone he called that Sunday (sans the final out) was the same one he had used his entire career, pointing out that he didn't have to eject anyone for arguing balls and strikes as his supporting evidence.

If it hadn't been for fortune, Hernandez doesn't pitch Game 5. And then someone other than Gregg is calling balls and strikes. And maybe Hernandez doesn't win. He almost certainly doesn't strike out fifteen; he averaged less than five a game during the regular season. He probably isn't awarded the MVP trophy. And who knows. Maybe the Marlins don't end up beating the Braves in six, going on to win the World Series over Cleveland.

And all of that makes Livan Hernandez Florida's very fortunate son.

Pine Tar
July 24 and August 18, 1983: Royals vs. Yankees

Only in New York could this theater of the absolute absurd have been believably played out. And only with this motley cast of true baseball characters.

Early in the 1983 regular season, during a game in Kansas City, Yankees third baseman Greg Nettles noticed the slathering of pine tar that covered the bat of George Brett beyond the allowed 18 inches. He pointed out the violation of baseball rules to his manager, Billy Martin, who then filed it away for use on a rainy day.

Martin's rainy day came on July 24 when Brett, facing Goose Gossage in the top of the ninth inning and trailing the Yankees 4-3, hit a 2-run lead-taking home run into the seats in right field.

Before Brett had even rounded first base, Martin had already sent one of his bat boys out to grab the adulterated bat in question. And just moments after Brett had given Kansas City a 1-run lead by touching home plate, the wily Martin had convened a meeting at the dish with rookie home plate umpire Tim McClelland and the rest of his crew.

As McClelland consulted the rulebook, and measured the bat's pine tar against the 17-inch home plate, Brett remembers sitting in the dugout and saying, "If they call me out for using too much pine tar I'm going to kill one of those SOBs." And true to his word, as soon as McClelland turned to the dugout

July 24, 1983: The Royals' George Brett goes ballistic when home plate umpire Tim McClelland wipes out his home run.

to signal Brett out, the Royals third baseman fired out of the dugout, raging like a crazed Tasmanian devil.

All chaos broke loose around the plate, with most of it centered around the effort to restrain the charging Brett, a task finally accomplished with a headlock from umpire Joe Brinkman. And while that was going on, the crafty veteran of rulebook violations, Gaylord Perry, snuck into the melee to grab the bat. But even though the umpires were busy with Brett, Yankee Stadium security was not, and they confiscated the bat from Perry, who was then summarily ejected by the umps.

Finally order was restored, and the Royals were forced to leave New York losers, leaving Martin to crow in the postgame press conference, "It turned out to be a lovely Sunday afternoon."

Not so fast, Billy.

In the ensuing days, Kansas City's protest landed on the desk of American League President Lee McPhail, who, despite his Manhattan address, ruled within the week to overturn McClelland's decision and reinstate Brett's home run. McPhail acknowledged that Brett's bat was illegal, but explained that he believed "games should be won and lost on the playing field—not through technicalities of the rules." Brett's bat, in his opinion, did not violate "the spirit of the rules" because pine tar does not make the ball travel farther.

Predictably the Yankees were outraged. And George Steinbrenner even quipped, "I wouldn't want to be Lee McPhail living in New York." But when the final four outs were rescheduled to be played three weeks later on August 18, an off-day for both teams, the Yankees showed up . . . sort of.

Center fielder Jerry Mumphrey, since traded to the Astros, was replaced in the field by starting pitcher Ron Guidry. Furthering the farce, Martin decided to move first baseman and left-handed thrower Don Mattingly to the uncomfortable position of second base. And then as play was just about to begin, Martin appealed at each base, claiming that the new set of umpires on hand for the twelve-minute affair couldn't possibly know if Brett had touched the bases back in July.

Anticipating the guileful Martin, crew chief Davey Phillips presented an affidavit that was signed by each member of the original umpiring crew, stating that Brett had indeed touched all four bases during his home-run trot. Martin then closed the curtain on the production by vociferously arguing until he was ejected from the game.

In response to the controversy, the official rulebook of Major League Baseball now notes: "If the umpire discovers that the bat does not conform to (c) above until a time during or after which the bat has been used in play, it shall not be grounds for declaring the batter out, or ejected from the game."

Amazin' Break

October 15, 1969: World Series Game 4, Orioles at Mets

Every season, without fail, controversy will envelop an otherwise routine ground ball when a batter runs to first base outside the designated three-foot lane and interferes with a fielder's throw to first. Its occurrence, and subsequent debate, is as regular as the seventh-inning stretch.

Is it fair to have the running lane on the foul side of the baseline, when the batter's natural momentum carries him into fair territory? Or when first base, the thing he's running toward, is also in fair ground?

Right or wrong, it's the rule. And never was it more discussed than after it was ignored in the 10th inning of Game 4 of the 1969 World Series.

To many, it's sacrilege to question the Amazin' Mets World Series run of 1969. As a new franchise in 1962, they lost 120 games. And from that expansion year (back when "expansion team" meant "decade-long doormat") through 1968, New York averaged 105 losses and never finished higher than ninth place. So not only was their '69 World Series championship improbable, it's been immortalized as legend on an Arthurian scale.

But we don't deal in myths or tread lightly around sacred cows. The reality is that in the 10th inning of Game 4, the Mets got a gift.

With the score tied 1-1 and two runners on (Rod Gasper at second and Al Weiss on first), pinch hitter J. C. Martin laid down a sacrifice bunt up the first-base line. Baltimore pitcher Pete Richert was quick off the mound to field the ball, but when he threw it to first base, the ball struck Martin on the wrist and bounced into right field, allowing Gasper to come all the way around from second to score the winning run.

Baseball Rule 7.09 (k) clearly states that the runner must have both feet within the three-foot lane along the first-base line, which Martin didn't. And if while outside of these lines, the runner interferes with the throw to first base—and interference doesn't get more clear-cut than having the ball actually hit you—then he is out, the ball is dead, and the other runners must return to their original bases.

Home plate umpire Shag Crawford, a man who worked a total of fourteen World Series games during his career, didn't see it that way. Crawford let the play stand as an error on Richert and a win for the Mets. A win that put them up three games to one and setting New York up for a Series-clinching win at Shea Stadium the following day.

Ironically, Crawford was also responsible for robbing baseball fans of what surely would have been an all-time classic confrontation. Baltimore manager Earl Weaver, one of the game's great showmen, wasn't around by the 10th inning to argue the decisive call because he'd been ejected by Crawford earlier in the game for arguing balls and strikes.

The Miracle Mets were indeed Amazin'. Tom Seaver and Jerry Koosman pitched brilliantly in Games 4 and 5. Series MVP Donn Clendenon, who actually turned down contract offers from the Cleveland Browns and Harlem Globetrotters to instead play baseball, hit three home runs in four games. And Tommie Agee's Game 3, in which he homered off Jim Palmer and made two spectacular catches in the outfield to strand five Baltimore runners, will forever stand as one of baseball's greatest single-game performances.

But when passing out praise for baseball's most celebrated underdog story, don't forget a helping for the man called Shag.

Bonehead Burden

September 23, 1908: Cubs at Giants

During the bottom of the ninth inning battle between the New York Knights Roy Hobbs and the Pirates young pitcher John Rhoades ("Nebraska farm boy, blazing left-handed speed"), sportswriter Max Mercy is already working on his "Hobbs as Goat" cartoon for the next morning's paper. In Mercy's own words, he's there to "protect this game." And he does it by "making or breaking the likes of [Hobbs]."

He tells Hobbs before the one-game playoff starts, "Whether you're a goat or a hero, you're going to make me a great story."

We of course all remember that in the end, Hobbs—dutiful, honorable, noble, and "the best there ever was"—was a hero. But for a full century of baseball now, the story has been the opposite for Fred Merkle. He is the ultimate goat, the definition of dunderhead, the craftsman of the ever-infamous "Merkle Boner" and its lifelong victim.

On the morning of September 23, 1908, the Giants regular first baseman, Fred Tenney, woke up with back spasms. So, unable to fill out his preferred lineup card for the all-important game against the second-place Cubs (trailing the Giants by mere percentage points), Hall of Fame manager John McGraw was forced to give nineteen-year-old Fred Merkle his first-ever start. A lucky break for a young and promising ballplayer, and one that Merkle would spend the rest of his life wishing he could give back.

For eight and a half innings no one paid Merkle any notice at first base. It was a pitcher's duel between future Hall of Famer Christy Mathewson and Cubs lefty Jack Pfiester, and Merkle's three previous at bats from the seventh spot had failed to bear fruit. But with two outs in the bottom of the ninth of a 1-1 game, and with left fielder Moose McCormick standing on first base, the young Merkle lashed a single into right field that sent McCormick to third with the potential game-winning run. And when the following batter, shortstop Al Bridwell, followed Merkle's single with a hit of his own, the 25,000 fans at the Polo Grounds swarmed the field in celebration.

McCormick strolled home with the Giants' winning run, while Merkle, who made it about halfway to second base before

McCormick crossed the plate, changed his course and began heading to the centerfield clubhouse—a critical decision that set in motion a laundry list of enduring controversies.

In the moments of confusion that followed, and surrounded by a crowd of fans that were also making their way to centerfield to exit the ballpark, Cubs future Hall of Fame second baseman Johnny Evers noticed that Merkle had failed to touch second base. According to the letter of baseball's laws, the force out was still in play, the inning was still technically alive, and the run hadn't officially counted yet. But that was only according to the letter of the law. Much like today's "area double-play" that allows for the middle infielder to record the out without actually touching second base, in 1908 it was protocol to immediately leave the field when a "walk off" hit (the annoyingly overused phrase wouldn't be coined until 1988) ended a game. Merkle was just following accepted practice.

Evers, though, was a desperate man not wanting to leave any stone unturned, so he retrieved the ball, then stepped on second base. (Some say that the ball Evers was holding when he touched second came from the Cubs dugout because the originally hit ball had been tossed into the stands by Giants future Hall of Fame pitcher Joe McGinnity—a fact he swore to. Others allege that Cubs pitcher Rube Kroh corralled the correct ball by actually punching out a fan who had refused to give it back after picking it up from the field.)

Whatever the case, Evers, with ball in hand, appealed the play to umpire Bob Emslie. But since he hadn't seen the play and refused to make a call, Evers took his case to home plate umpire Hank O'Day, where he found a friendly ruling. Merkle was declared out, the run was taken off the board, and since the field was teeming with fans, the game was called a draw, 1-1. (It's rumored, but impossible to confirm, that earlier in the season Evers had had a similar appeal to O'Day regarding a force play on a game-winning hit denied.)

When the Giants were notified in the clubhouse that their victory had been invalidated, they were naturally outraged. And after National League President Harry Pulliam upheld O'Day's decision, which was further validated by a baseball board of directors' meeting on October 5, several members of the team refused to play the one-game playoff with Chicago resulting from their season-ending 98-55 identical records. The Giants' reasoning was simple: they'd already played, and won.

Eventually the group of players, led by Mathewson, relented, and the game was played on October 8. But defeat had already come to New York. Chicago's 4-2 win that claimed its third straight National League pennant was merely a formality.

Many of the details of what Merkle was doing during the madcap final moments have been lost in the legend that followed. Stories range from Merkle claiming that he actually did go back and touch the base, to umpire Bob Emslie telling him he didn't have to. The one man who knew for sure, however, never talked about it. The incident and subsequent label of "bonehead" so shook the young ballplayer—Merkle actually contemplated retirement at age nineteen—that he refused to speak about it for the rest of his sixty-seven-year life.

Join us in ending the prevailing myth of Merkle's Boner, and place the blame where it fairly lies: at the feet of umpire Hank O'Day.

The Fenway Phantom Tag

October 16, 1999: ALCS Game 4, Yankees at Red Sox

The *American Heritage Dictionary* defines the word *phantom* as "something apparently seen, heard, or sensed, but having no physical reality." And that's exactly how Red Sox fans define Chuck Knoblauch's "phantom tag" in Game 4 of the 1999 ALCS.

When it comes to the Yankees, it doesn't take much to get

under the skin of Bostonians. Remember when a loutish Yankee fan visiting Boston was attacked by rabid n devotee Carla Tortelli, putting Sam Malone in jeopardy of losing his bar in a lawsuit? And that was fiction. Which, incidentally, is how everyone in Fenway Park the night of October 16 would probably describe the first out in the bottom of the eighth.

This game had it all, including Yankees reliever Jeff Nelson going after a Fenway Park security guard for trying to protect him—not to be confused with Nelson's attack on a Fenway Park groundskeeper four years later, for which he was sued—and angry Sox fans pelting the field with bottles. Of course they'll tell you that they were provoked by umpire Tom Tschida.

This particular crazy chapter in the ongoing Yankees-Red Sox saga began in the bottom of the eighth with the Red Sox trailing by 1. With Jose Offerman on first and no outs, John Valentin hit a slow roller to Knoblauch at second base. Fielding the ball, Knoblauch made a futile swipe at the passing Offerman before firing the ball to first base for the single, sure out.

But even though Knoblauch's tag missed Offerman by a good three feet, Tom Tschida called him out, completing the double play and killing the Red Sox rally.

You have to rewind back to the 10th inning of Game 1, when Knoblauch was given credit for a force-out by umpire Rick Reed—also involving Offerman—as the ball was coming out of his glove for what should have been an error, to get the full measure of the pain felt in Fenway Park that night. As the fans saw it, Knoblauch was now the beneficiary of two blown calls; and both robbed them of wins. And providing absolutely no measure of comfort for anyone in Boston, both Reed and Tschida would later admit that the calls should have gone the other way.

Feeling eighty-one years of frustration, the Sox fans lost it. And they spent the remainder of the game lobbing anything and everything onto the field of play, putting the Yankees, and their own beloved Red Sox, at serious risk for injury.

The grave situation was given a modicum of levity thanks to funnyman George Steinbrenner. After the game the Yankees owner put the blame for the fans' behavior squarely on the shoulders of Boston manager Jimy Williams, claiming that when Williams was arguing the blown call, and he kicked the dirt and threw his hat, he was in fact trying to incite the fans. (Steinbrenner, of course, would never employ a hat-throwing, dirt-kicking manager.)

And then when the reporter's questions turned specifically to the blown call du jour, Steinbrenner delivered his funniest line since, and including, his appearance on Saturday Night Live, keeping a straight face and answering, "Those things happen. I never complain about umpires' calls."

Herbie's Heft

October 20, 1991: World Series Game 2, Braves at Twins

At the risk of undoing centuries of male concentrated persuasion to the contrary, and in the process crush the prospective promise of millions of our fellow men, it is time to come clean. Size does matter. It matters in basketball, where a 7-foot-7 Manute Bol can go from Dinka herdsman to NBA dunk master. It matters in football, where a man's physical similarities to a refrigerator can take him from the buffet line to across the Super Bowl goal line. And it matters in baseball, where, depending on the umpire, it's okay to use one's boundless ballast to remove an opponent from first base.

It was perhaps the most unlikely World Series matchup in baseball history. Both the Twins and Braves just one year earlier in 1990 were last-place finishers. But by 1991 the two teams were going toe-to-toe in what was arguably the best World Series ever, punctuated by Kirby Puckett's 11th inning walk-off home run in Game 6 and by Jack Morris's ten shutout innings in Game 7.

How great was this series? And just how small side's margin for error?

Three games went into extra innings, including Game 6 and Game 7. Three games ended with the winning run scoring on the final pitch. Four games ended with the winning run coming in the team's final at bat. And five of the seven games were decided by just one run.

And of course, it also had controversy.

Following a Game 1 Minnesota win—where Morris got the first of his two wins—Atlanta went into Game 2 still hoping to get the early road split. And in the top of the third, and down by 1, Ron Gant seemed to get a Braves rally started with a line-drive hit to left.

Like every other single Gant hit during his sixteen-year career, he rounded first base. And like 99.9% of the time when he rounded first base, he was forced to return to the bag after the outfielder handled the ball cleanly and threw it back into the infield.

There was absolutely no drama at all when Gant got back to the bag ahead of the throw and first baseman Kent Hrbek's tag. He beat the play easily. But when the force of the 250-pound Hrbek's sweeping tag knocked the 170-pound Gant's leg up and off the base, umpire Drew Coble immediately called Gant out.

An argument naturally ensued, but Coble, who was standing behind the play and shielded by Hrbek's hefty frame, held firm. He said that it was Gant's momentum that had carried him off the bag, and not Hrbek, an opinion that Coble continued to sell years later, even though all angles of the television replay proved it dubious at best.

The Braves went on to lose the game 3-2. And in the process of dropping the series in seven, Atlanta lost two more games by just one run.

Braves fans, who to this day refer to the Metrodome as "The Scene of the Crime," spent Games 3, 4, and 5 in Atlanta making harassing and threatening phone calls to Hrbek's hotel room.

Turn the Other Cheek

October 14, 1978: World Series Game 4, Dodgers at Yankees

The mid to late 1970s should have been a tranquil time for everyone in Yankees pinstripes. George Steinbrenner, promising to be a hands-off owner, had taken the reins in 1973. And after a pennant in 1976 and the franchise's first World Series win in fifteen years in 1977, peace, harmony, and happiness should have reigned supreme.

But this team had Billy Martin as manager, a boastful barroom brawler who would later lose a job for punching out a marshmallow salesman; Reggie Jackson, the self-proclaimed "straw that stirs the drink"; and the hands-off Steinbrenner (stifled laugh), who was coming off a suspension for illegally contributing to Richard Nixon's re-election campaign and obstructing justice—although "The Boss" would eventually get a presidential pardon from "The Gipper" in 1989, one day before Ronald Reagan left office.

In July of 1978—a year after a very public dugout blowup between Martin and Jackson was seen on national television, prompting Steinbrenner, who was no longer sticking "to building ships," to seek his manager's replacement—Martin told the New York Times that Jackson and Steinbrenner deserved each other because "one's a born liar and the other's been convicted."

Martin was predictably forced to resign—the first of seventeen managerial changes by Steinbrenner (four involving Martin) over the next fifteen years—and by the time the Yankees made it back to the World Series that October, Bob Lemon was at the helm.

That takes us to the night of October 14, and Game 4 at Yankee Stadium.

With the Dodgers leading the Series 2 games to 1, and up 3-1 in the sixth inning, the Yankees' situation looked bleak. And when Lou Piniella hit what appeared to be an inning-ending double play with Jackson on first base, fans in L.A. began to think ahead to a possible series-clinching Game 5.

But as shortstop Bill Russell stepped on second base to force out Jackson, Mr. October showed everyone that he could swing more than just a big bat on baseball's biggest stage—he also could swing a big backside.

Intentionally heaving his hulking right hip into the passing baseball, Jackson sent the throw catapulting off into right field, scoring Thurman Munson from second base. The Dodgers, blue in the face, argued the play vehemently, claiming a clear case of runner's interference. But instead of calling Piniella out, taking Munson's run off the board, and ending the inning, the umpires—no doubt picturing a night in the Bronx with 50,000 angry Yankees fans—let the play stand.

The Yankees would go on to tie the game 3-3 on Munson's double in the eighth. And then, after two scoreless innings pitched by Goose Gossage, New York tied the series 2-2 on a legitimate hit by Piniella in the 10th.

The shell-shocked Dodgers lost the final two games by a combined score of 19-4.

In 1981 Los Angeles would exact its pound of flesh by beating the Yankees in six games, and hanging an 0-for-5 with two strikeouts on Jackson in his final career World Series game.

Eddings's Erring Eyes

October 12, 2005: ALCS Game 2, Angels at White Sox

It wasn't exactly the Black Sox of 1919, and "Say it ain't so, Joe." And we aren't advocating that a Kenesaw Mountain Landis–type character come in and suspend anyone from the game for life. But the White Sox World Series win of 2005, their first since 1917, did include a black mark because of one of the men in blue: Doug Eddings.

Heading into the ALCS against the Los Angeles Angels of Anaheim (of Southern California in the United States of

America of the Western Hemisphere), most baseball observers wondered which White Sox team would show up: The club that had just swept the defending champion Red Sox in the Division Series; or the team that had struggled down the stretch, played .500 baseball after July, and had just suffered a home September three-game sweep at the hands of the Angels.

Early on, it looked like we had our answer. Despite losing in New York on Sunday night, flying back to California for an ALDS deciding win on Monday night (plus celebration), and then taking a red-eye flight to Chicago for Game 1 against the Sox on Tuesday night, the bleary-eyed Angels took the series opener 3-2.

And things didn't get much better for Chicago's bats the second night, playing the Angels to a 1-1 draw through eight and a half innings.

With two outs and two strikes in the bottom of the ninth, Sox catcher A. J. Pierzynski swung and missed at Kelvim Escobar's delivery for strike three. And an unmistakable "out" signal from home plate umpire Doug Eddings appeared to send the game into the 10th inning—until suddenly Pierzynski, who had already taken a couple of steps toward Chicago's third-base-line dugout, reversed direction and instead ran to first.

Looking confused, even though he claimed afterward that he had the call the entire way, Eddings appeared to reverse direction too, ruling that Angels catcher Josh Paul did not catch the ball cleanly. Poor Paul just happened to be the only unlucky soul involved in the play that couldn't reverse himself. He'd already rolled the ball irretrievably back toward the pitching mound.

So instead of a third out, it was a dropped third strike, and the White Sox had new life. New life that led to an easy steal of second base by pinch runner Pablo Ozuna, who then scored on a game-winning double by the next batter up, Joe Crede.

The Angels couldn't get over losing their chance to take a 2-0

Game 2, 2005 ALCS: Angels catcher Josh Paul catches strike three, but umpire Doug Eddings ruled that he dropped it.

series lead, and ended up losing the next three games, and the series, by a combined score of 19-7.

Eddings—who refused to admit that he blew the play and helped the White Sox steal a critical win, but did acknowledge that the raised, clenched fist he uses to signal "strike" is very similar to his "out" call, and may have been confusing to Paul—has become the source of Internet income for the enterprising owner of FireDougEddings.com, where membership comes complete with T-shirt and bumper sticker.

Sleight of Hand
October 1, 2007: NL Wildcard 1-Game Playoff, Padres at Rockies

Just like your mother always said, two wrongs do not make a right.

And for the scientific proof that mom was making a statement of fact and not simply moralizing, let's look no further than her other favorite homilies.

If given enough time, gravity and the Earth's rotation ensure that what goes around does eventually come around. Top theologians meeting recently at a multi-denominational conference in Rome determined that idle hands are in fact the location of the devil's playground. And be honest, didn't you judge this book by its cover, just a little?

So with the wisdom of mom clearly in our corner, the terrible safe call on Matt Holliday in the bottom of the 13th inning of the Padres-Rockies one-game playoff should not be written off as inconsequential because the Rockies were robbed of a run earlier in the game. The ends do not justify the means (it's no coincidence that this philosophy comes from Machiavelli, whose name has since become an adjective for deceptive and dishonest behavior), and two bad umpire's calls do not equal baseball justice.

We do not claim that San Diego should have been the National League's wildcard team. The Padres had three cracks at a postseason clinching win to finish out the regular season, failing each time. They then had a fourth chance lost when Cooperstown-bound Trevor Hoffman started throwing batting practice during Colorado's half of the 13th.

On the other side, the Rockies won 14 of 15 games to get themselves into the extra game with San Diego. The Rockies then proved they belonged in the postseason by sweeping past the Phillies and Diamondbacks and making their first ever trip to the World Series.

The team that deserved to win did. There was no better story in baseball in 2007 than Colorado's meteoric climb to claim the wildcard. Rudy gets the sack in his final game at Notre Dame. Jimmy Chitwood makes the shot to give Hickory the Indiana State Championship. And the Rockies beat the Padres in the final game of the extended regular season.

It just would have been nice if they didn't win on a terrible call.

If you're a baseball fan, you remember the scene. Back-to-back doubles by Kaz Matsui and Troy Tulowitzki, followed by Matt Holliday's triple, erased San Diego's two-run lead and put the winning run for Colorado just 90 feet away for the .225 hitting Jamey Carroll. He then lofted a shallow fly ball to right field that Brian Giles fielded on the run and heaved home to try and get the sprinting Holliday.

As Holliday approached the plate and began his dive he appeared to have a clean shot at it, with Padres catcher Michael Barrett favoring the first base side. But just as Barrett fielded Giles's throw, he swung his left foot over to block the plate from Holliday's outstretched hand—successfully. Holliday slid past the plate, never touching it, and after Barrett secured the ball he applied the tag.

Holliday, perhaps dazed from his face plant in the dirt, or because he knew that he never touched home, had no reaction. The on-deck batter had no reaction, perhaps because he saw that Holliday failed to score. And home plate umpire Tim McClelland (the same Tim McClelland who called George Brett out because of too much pine tar) had virtually no reaction until meekly signaling Holliday safe.

On the definitive call of an extra inning play-in game, at the very least you would expect some emotion. An emphatic and repeated safe call or directed pointing at the plate—something assertive—would have indicated that McClelland saw it get touched by Holliday. But we got nothing.

What we got instead was McClelland, the next day in an

interview with *The Des Moines Register*, saying, "Watching replay later, I had a little doubt. But if I had to call it again, I'd call it the same way."

And it would be the wrong call, again.

The replays of the play are not inconclusive just because home plate is obscured. It didn't disappear or change locations just because Barrett's body was blocking its view. Holliday's hand and the plate were still both there. And we can still conclude that the two objects failed to make contact with each other, even if we have to use the leap of logic that the plate didn't move.

The good news out of all of this is that baseball seems to be getting the message that bad calls are just that—bad. And that technology in the 21st century is in fact good. A little over a month after Holliday's sleight of hand, baseball's general managers voted 25-5 to recommend the use of instant replay on disputed home run calls. That wouldn't have made a difference on the Holliday call—it doesn't fall within the parameters of instant replay. But it would have been used on the disputed Garrett Atkins home run to left (he stopped at second with a double) that appeared to bounce back into the field only after clearing the fence and hitting a wheelchair in the stands.

If that play were to be overturned, as it should have, then the extra innings never happen and the Rockies win without the aid of Tim McClelland.

Of course, that's assuming that replay would have overturned the non–home run call. When asked about the replays of Atkins's home run that wasn't, McClelland told the *Register*, "I don't think anyone could truly say for sure that it 100% left the ballpark."

And that is why even replay will never 100% stop bad umpiring.

If you ever stop to say, "What's going to happen to me if I make this call," you might as well take your whistle and shove it, because that's all the respect you're giving it.

EARL STROM

NBA AND ABA REFEREE (1957–1990)

You wanna know the chief quality a ref has gotta have in the NBA? That's a pair of elephant balls.

JASON WILLIAMS

NBA POINT GUARD

What does it take to be a good referee? Beats the hell out of me. No one thinks any referee is good.

RICHIE POWERS

NBA REFEREE (1956–1979)

NBA AND COLLEGE
BASKETBALL

When Dr. James Naismith was charged with creating a game of skill that would give his rowdy class of boys an indoor "athletic distraction" during a particularly brutal New England winter in 1891, it's doubtful he envisioned that "basket ball" (played initially with a soccer ball and peach baskets) would turn into the phenomenon played today by more than 300 million people worldwide.

It began with thirteen rudimentary rules. There was no dribbling, only passes from "the open spot on which a [player] catches [the ball]." Two fouls on a player would disqualify him from the game (no substitutions) until the next basket was made. Three consecutive team fouls resulted in a basket for the other team. And there was absolutely no punching at the ball with a closed fist. That also resulted in a foul.

In fact, of all the major team sports in America, today's basketball resembles its nineteenth-century roots the least. And some might say that today's NBA game follows its own current set of rules less than any other professional sport. Rule 12, Part B, Section 1 reads:

> *A player shall not hold, push, charge into, or impede the*
> *progress of an opponent by extending a hand, forearm, leg*
> *or knee.*

Absent from this rule, or the twelve sections in the rules regarding traveling, is any mention of an opt-out exception for superstars. *Officially* Patrick Ewing's patented bunny-hop post move was a traveling violation. Palming the ball and pushing off, even when your name is Michael Jordan and you drink Gatorade, is *technically* against the rules. And just because a center wears a size-21 shoe and weighs 330 pounds, he does not have to bleed from multiple lacerations before a foul is called.

So recognizing that there hasn't been an NBA game that's followed the absolute letter of the law in more than forty years, we won't waste your time with *those* bad calls. We're only concerned with the especially egregious mistakes that changed championship fortunes or displayed outrageously bad judgment.

NBA

Hue Hollins's Helping Hand

May 18, 1994: Eastern Conference Semifinals Game 5, Bulls at Knicks

Conventional wisdom among the cynical sect of basketball fans says that Scottie Pippen emerged from his seventeen-year career overrated and unworthy of inclusion among the NBA's 50 Greatest Players. After all, he never won a championship without Michael Jordan.

But Magic Johnson never won without Kareem Abdul-Jabbar. Larry Bird didn't win without Robert Parish. Julius Erving shared his one championship with Moses Malone. And if you want to get technical, Jordan never won without Pippen. Yet Magic, Bird, Dr. J, and MJ never had to battle the shadow

Game 5, 1994 Eastern Conference Semifinals: Scottie Pippen is called for a foul on Hubert Davis's final shot.

of a great teammate and the perceptions of undeserved coattail riding the way Pippen has.

Pippen did bring much of the disrespect upon himself. He took himself out of an important playoff game when coach Phil Jackson drew up a final shot for Toni Kukoc, and not him. He often complained about his contract with his bosses in Chicago. In Houston, he had very public run-ins with Charles Barkley. And in Portland, even though he took the Blazers to the playoffs each of the four years he was there, the last three were first-round exits.

But maybe if Pippen had managed to eke out just one championship in Jordan's absence—or even a trip to the finals—the conflicts and complaints that color his career would instead be seen as acts of a competitive veteran leader. Michael Jordan once punched out Steve Kerr during a Bulls practice, but he didn't become a "malcontent." In the eyes of the fans and media, Jordan was simply that driven to win. An occasional blowup was quickly forgiven because of who he was.

Pippen's best chance to "be like Mike" came when the aforementioned Gatorade poster boy spent a humbling year playing Mendoza Line baseball for the Birmingham Barons. During that season (1993–94) Pippen led the Bulls to a 55-27 record (just two fewer wins than with Jordan the year before), he was the All-Star Game MVP, averaged a career-high 22 ppg, and finished third in regular season MVP balloting. With Michael Jordan immersed in a favored rich man's baseball fantasy camp, the Bulls and Phil Jackson needed a new leader. Scottie Pippen seamlessly filled that role.

In the playoffs, and taking on the Knicks in the Eastern Conference Semifinals, the Bulls were leading Game 5, 86-85, with just seconds to play. A win would give them a critical victory on the road, a 3 games to 2 series lead, and a chance to clinch a trip to the conference finals back home in Chicago.

With the clock ticking down, and unable to shake Pippen, one of the game's best defenders, New York's Hubert Davis was forced to throw up a 20-foot game-ending prayer just inches over Pippen's long reach. The shot clanked harmlessly off the rim and it appeared that Chicago had just taken the pivotal Game 5—until the whistle of referee Hue Hollins broke the tension, as well as the long-standing NBA philosophy of not calling ticky-tack fouls in the closing seconds of playoff games.

Pippen did bump Davis following the shot. That's not in dispute. But at the very moment that Davis released the ball, and Pippen nearly blocked it, a good three feet still separated the two. Is that a foul? And more importantly, a foul with 2.1 seconds left in the fourth quarter of a playoff game? The objective answer in the very subjective world of NBA refereeing is no.

In this case, however, it was. And it was Davis's two gifted free throws that proved the difference in the Knicks' 87-86 win.

Had the foul on Pippen not been called, the Bulls had an excellent chance of advancing to the Eastern Conference Finals instead of losing to New York in seven games as they did. And if, at a minimum, they'd advanced as far as the Knicks did that year—runner up to Houston in the NBA Finals—maybe even the cynics would recognize Scottie Pippen as one of the game's great players.

Four-Point Favoritism

June 5, 1999: Eastern Conference Finals Game 3, Pacers at Knicks

For years now, legions of conspiracy theorists have fixated on the NBA like UFO nut jobs on Roswell, New Mexico. The league's office at Olympic Tower on Fifth Avenue is their grassy knoll. Commissioner David Stern is the head of the Illuminati. And the NBA draft lottery is sports' portrayal of NASA's fabricated moon landing.

The theory goes that the "black helicopters" of the NBA draft lottery were launched in 1985 so that the Knicks, not coincidentally the team in the country's biggest television market, could land college basketball's biggest and most recognizable star, Patrick Ewing. And it was that newly created system (previously a coin toss between last-place teams had been used) and one carefully orchestrated bounce of a ping-pong ball that took New York from occasional playoff participant to perennial championship contender.

And with these theorists fervently following the famous direction of distinguished conspiracy whistleblower Deep

Throat—"Follow the money"— they happily note that in 1985 the NBA's combined cable and network television contracts paid the league just over $111 million. In 1994, the season the Knicks used an assist from Hue Hollins to beat the Bulls and make the NBA Finals, the television money was up to $876 million. The very next season, in negotiations that were no doubt aided by television ratings inflated by a New York playoff audience, the league signed a deal for $1.29 billion.

The current contract set to expire in 2008 is worth $4.6 billion.

The devotees of the dogma also like to point out that 21 of the 27 NBA Finals played between 1980 and 2006 featured a team from New York (including New Jersey), Los Angeles, or Chicago—the three largest television markets in the country. And when comparing that 78% to the NFL's (22%), MLB's (40%), and NHL's (44%) big-three-market success, for them it becomes a little less loony to leap to conspiracy.

For those that believe the league and its officials influence who wins, who loses, and who tunes in to television, Exhibit A of the NBA's New York state of mind is the drafting of Patrick Ewing. Exhibit B is Hue Hollins's call on Scottie Pippen. And because all things in comedy and conspiracy must conclude in threes, there is the four-point "magic bullet" by the Knicks' Larry Johnson.

It was Game 3 of the 1999 Eastern Conference Finals between New York and Indiana (television market #25). And with the series tied 1-1 and the Pacers up 91-88, the Knicks were in danger of dropping a pivotal game at home. Late in the fourth quarter Pacers center Rick Smits had rattled off six straight points, and with just 11.9 seconds left, guard Mark Jackson sank a pair of free throws to push the lead to three and put New York firmly on the ropes.

Playing for a final shot, and in obvious need of a 3-pointer, Johnson was getting in position to take the game-ender when he was fouled by Indiana's Antonio Davis with just 5.7 seconds to play. Referee Jess Kersey's whistle blew, and then, nearly a full second later, Johnson released a shot that went in. But in what can only be described as the most liberal interpretation of "continuation" in NBA playoff history, Kersey shocked the arena by raising his arms to signal the basket good (tying the game) and award Johnson a follow-up free throw (to win it).

LJ's "miracle" four-point play, as described by *The New York Times*, put the Knicks up in the series 2 games to 1 and helped them become the first-ever eighth seed to advance to the NBA Finals, where they eventually lost to the Spurs in five games.

We espouse that there was nothing at play in the Garden that Saturday more sinister than Kersey's bad judgment. And for the Pacers, that was plenty sinister enough. But for the cabal of foolhardy conspiracy crazies, "Warren Commission"-er David Stern's denials simply fueled their cause.

Tinseltown Treachery
May 31, 2002: Western Conference Finals Game 6, Kings at Lakers

Dear Mr. Stern,

At a time when the public's confidence is shaken by headlines reporting the breach of trust by corporate executives, it is important, during the public's relaxation time, for there to be maintained a sense of impartiality and professionalism in commercial sports performances. That sense was severely shaken in the now notorious officiating during Game 6 of the Western Conference Finals between the Los Angeles Lakers and the Sacramento Kings.

It seems that you have a choice. You can continue to exercise your absolute power to do nothing. Or you can initiate a review and if all these observers and fans turn out to be right, issue, together with the referees, an apology to the Sacramento Kings and forthrightly admit decisive incompetence during Game 6, especially in the crucial fourth quarter.

No government in our country can lawfully stifle free speech and fine those who exercise it; the NBA under present circumstances can both stifle and fine players and coaches who speak up. There is no guarantee that this tyrannical status quo will remain stable over time, should you refuse to bend to reason and the reality of what occurred. A review that satisfies the fans' sense of fairness and deters future recurrences would be a salutary contribution to the public trust that the NBA badly needs. We look forward to your considered response.

Sincerely,
Ralph Nader

While most people wouldn't call the NBA "tyrannical," as Ralph Nader did in 2002 in this abridged version of his 825-word letter to commissioner David Stern—taking him from the ho-hum life of consumer rights advocate and three-time presidential candidate to the much more gratifying world of NBA watchdog—everyone was in agreement about the embarrassment that passed for officiating in the Lakers' Game 6 win over Sacramento. Officiating that cost Sacramento a trip to the NBA Finals.

Phil Jackson, the winning Lakers coach, said, "The Kings deserved to win."

Longtime hoops coach Rick Majerus was so moved by the injustice of Game 6 that he wrote an op-ed in the *Los Angeles Times* that called out the NBA's unwritten but widely recognized double standard for stars like Kobe Bryant and Shaquille O'Neal.

Washington Post columnist Michael Wilbon wrote that many of the calls in the fourth quarter were "stunningly incorrect," and that he has "never seen officiating in a game of consequence as bad as that in Game 6."

And David Dupree of *USA Today* said, "I've been covering the NBA for thirty years, and it's the poorest officiating in an important game I've ever seen."

The issues with the job referees Bob Delaney, Dick Bevetta, and Ted Bernhardt did in the most universally recognized fleecing in playoff history are many. Kings big man Scot Pollard fouled out early in the fourth quarter on a play during which he didn't so much as touch Shaquille O'Neal. Center Vlade Divac picked up his sixth and final foul while chasing a 50/50 loose ball on the floor, joking after the game, "It was my turn." And the Lakers, who had been averaging just 22 foul shots a game in the series, made it to the line 27 times in the fourth quarter alone.

In stark contrast to the quick whistles that were bleeding Sacramento to an agonizingly slow playoff death, a late Kobe Bryant elbow that left the nose of Mike Bibby battered and bloodied fell outside the capricious parameters of a foul as momentarily defined by this threesome of officials.

In the fourth quarter the Lakers offense made all of five baskets. But with 21 points coming from the stripe, L.A. was able to take the referee's gifted game, 106-102, survive elimination, and eventually win the series in a dramatic Game 7 overtime on the road in Sacramento.

But no one remembers that. Or the incredible last-second shot Robert Horry hit to win Game 4. Or Bibby's winning heroics at the end of Game 5.

No one remembers what a classic series the 2002 Western Conference Finals was, or why so much of what happened on the floors of Arco Arena and Staples Center during its seven-game war defines what we love about NBA playoff basketball. But to a fan— casual to crazed, Lakers, Kings, and otherwise uncommitted— everyone remembers the shameful sham that was Game 6.

And the next time you cast a ballot for President of the United

States, remember that even if you don't agree with Ralph Nader on corporate tax shifts, electoral reform, and decentralized democracy, come playoff time Ralph's got your back.

Boston Garden Sun Set
June 4, 1976: NBA Finals Game 5, Suns at Celtics

Every sport has that one game that stands out as a timeless classic. A definitive meeting that ends up endowing permanent change en masse upon the players involved, while elevating the sport to new heights in the consciousness of the casual fan.

For the NFL that game was the 1958 NFL Championship between the Colts and Giants, an overtime thriller (the NFL's first) under the lights of Yankee Stadium that started Johnny Unitas on the road to Canton, Ohio. Tennis fans who saw the 1980 Wimbledon Final between John McEnroe and Bjorn Borg will never forget Mac's 18-16 marathon tiebreaker win in the fourth set. It almost didn't matter that he went on to lose the title to Borg in the fifth. And the Mets' electrifying 6-5 ten-inning win in Game 6 of the 1986 World Series will forever define the vacillating highs and lows and the accompanying anguish of October baseball.

The NBA's version of the game that had everything—heroes, villains, and miracles—is Game 5 of the 1976 Finals between the Suns and Celtics.

With the series tied 2-2, and so far trending to the home court, the Celtics built an early 22-point lead on the famed parquet floor of venerable Boston Garden. But the upstarts from Phoenix, who had shocked their way past the defending champion Blazers in the Western Conference Finals, battled back gamely, erasing the deficit in the closing seconds of the fourth quarter to force overtime.

The back-and-forth action continued in the extra period, and with the score knotted up at 101 and a second overtime looming,

Celtics star Paul Silas called a timeout with three seconds left to set up a final shot for Boston.

Incidentally, it was a timeout the Celtics didn't have.

As was demonstrated by Michigan's Chris Webber seventeen years later, calling a timeout that you do not have results in a championship-losing technical foul. But in this case, despite the clear-as-day rules not subject to interpretation, and the desperate pleas of everyone wearing Phoenix Suns attire, referee Richie Powers ignored Silas's request and instead allowed the clock to expire. No timeout. No technical foul. And no free throw attempt for Phoenix to win the game.

The second overtime ended with even more craziness. Boston's John Havlicek sank an apparent game-winning shot that prompted a frenzied storming of the court. But as determined by Powers, one second still remained on the clock, and now down by 1, the Suns would get a final chance, a decision that incited one angry Celtics fan to attack the very man who'd kept Boston alive with his earlier no-call as he tried to clear the floor.

In the pandemonium of the moment, Phoenix's Paul Westphal came up with a plan: call a timeout specifically *because* the Suns didn't have any left. This time, of course, the technical foul was called. The Celtics hit the resulting free throw to extend their lead to 2, but Westphal's stroke of strategic inspiration set Phoenix up at mid-court for the inbounds pass, instead of from under their basket. And that set up Gar Heard for his improbable buzzer-beating basket, which took everyone to an exhausting third overtime.

An overtime that saw the Suns' heroics finally come to an end and the Celtics escape with a 128-126 win.

The Suns had already beaten the Celtics twice in the series in Phoenix, and it's only a small step to assume that had Powers made the right call and Paul Westphal made the technical foul free throw—he shot 83% from the line that year—Phoenix would have been the NBA champions of 1976.

Instead, the drained and deflated Suns lost two nights later, 87-80, and Boston captured its thirteenth world title.

Westphal said years later that he saw Silas call the timeout, "and so did Richie Powers."

And for his part in "The Greatest Game Ever Played," as first penned by *Phoenix Gazette* columnist Joe Gilmartin, Silas never denied his role as almsman to Powers's Daddy Warbucks, admitting, "I tried to call [timeout] and Richie Powers didn't see me, or didn't want to see me."

For the explanation as to what exactly Silas meant by "didn't want to see me," we have the alleged words of Powers himself: "I just couldn't see the Celtics losing that way, especially on their home court."

Following two separate incidents in 1978 in which he ignored the league's rules, including one that ironically involved the excessive assessment of three technical fouls to one player (two was the limit), Richie Powers was fired.

The Short Road to Replay
April 27, 2002: Eastern Conference Playoffs First Round Game 3, Hornets at Magic

The first-ever televised sporting event was a college baseball game between Princeton and Columbia in 1939, shot with a single camera angled up the third base line. Twenty-four years later, during the 1963 Army-Navy telecast, instant replay was first used. Twenty-three years after that innovation, the NFL became the first professional sports league to use instant replay to correct its erring officials.

The speed of advancing change was downright glacial.

By 2002, a full sixty-three years after sports first met television, which was followed by the advent of the sports bar, the arm-chair critic, and the rhetorical rail, "Did you see that terrible call?"

the NBA had failed to embrace the march of technology. The powers that be still embraced "the human element" of referees and the quaintness of the occasional blown call.

It bears mentioning that the majority of the players and fans did not share the league's avidness for the antiquated.

And neither did a majority of the owners after the "Baron Davis" incident on April 27.

Game 3 of the playoff series between the Orlando Magic and the Charlotte Hornets was tied 92-92 with just 0.7 seconds remaining. As Charlotte huddled together, planning a quick pass-and-shoot inbounds play for their talented point guard Davis, the referees, led by Bernie Fryer, held their own conference to discuss the final play.

Shortly after the assemblages broke up, P. J. Brown fired a quick pass to Davis, who in a split second caught, turned, and released. But as Davis's shot arched toward the basket on its way to an apparent game-winning 3-pointer, Fryer began blowing his whistle and waving his arms wildly. The basket would not count.

During the officials' muddle of their minds, Fryer took it upon himself to predetermine that 0.7 seconds was not enough time for anyone to catch the ball, then shoot it, because as Fryer later explained, "He had to cock it to get a 3-pointer up, to get muscle behind it, and I said you can't do that in seven-tenths. You can rely on the clock, but I'm going to rely on my judgment."

As it turned out, the clock would have been a much better way for Fryer to go. A replay of the final shot showed that not only did the clock start on time, which Fryer feared it would not, but Davis released the ball with 0.2 seconds still displayed, an indisputable fact prejudged to be an impossibility by Fryer.

Upon seeing the video evidence of his very poor decision, a contrite Fryer said, "Obviously, the way it ran in slow motion, I am probably wrong."

The damage was mitigated by the fact that Charlotte went on to win the game in overtime thanks to a pair of unquestioned 3-pointers by Davis. The fallout, however, was far reaching.

In July of 2002 the NBA's Board of Governors approved the use of instant replay on all controversial last-second shots, bravely breaching the bondage of yore and embracing the betterment of twenty-first-century progress.

The Wronging of Riles
December 19, 2002: NBA League Office

Why is it that in the world of sports officiating, the phrase "human error" has come to mean ill-timed blinks, eyes unfortunately focused on the wrong place, and the speed of play outpacing the quickness of cognition? It's as if all human errors are nothing more than accidents brought on by our own physical limitations.

But aren't all human beings also vindictive? Do we not hold grudges, often allowing our emotions to interfere with rational thought and the job at hand? Do we not naturally favor the things, people, and places that we like? While sometimes seeking to injure the people we don't?

Are we not petty?

That absolute pettiness played itself out in the case of Pat Riley vs. Steve Javie. Of course, everyone knows Pat Riley's name. He's coached in the third-most NBA Championships in history. But most of us also know Steve Javie's name. And for a league that boasts the best referees in the world and would prefer them to mostly remain anonymous—a strong indicator that they're good at their job—Javie's notoriety has to be troubling. Not to mention his behavior.

In December 2002, following a tough loss to the Knicks in which he spent much of the game battling the officials and watching his Heat shoot 21 fewer free throws, Riley told a

Heat head coach Pat Riley has a "discussion" with his nemesis, referee Steve Javie.

postgame press conference that the official's "hatred" for him was "unjust" and hurting his players. He then specifically called out Javie for an incident a year old, when Javie allegedly told Riley during a loss to Cleveland, "It's giving us absolute delight to watch you and your team die."

Ranting about the refs, of course, is a no-no. And because of his postgame tirade to the media, Riley was slapped with a $50,000 fine. But was Riley telling the truth?

"We're looking into it," was the terse response of NBA spokesman Mark Broussard.

At the very least, we already knew that Javie, a veteran ref with more than a dozen NBA Finals games to his credit, carries the very human trait of thin skin. During a game in 1991 he ejected the mascot of the Washington Bullets, Hoop. Then three years later he ejected the radio analyst of the Portland Trail Blazers, Mike Rice, for criticizing his calls during a broadcast. It's believed to be the only time that a courtside broadcaster has been removed from a game and escorted from the arena at the direction of an NBA referee.

Two months after Riley made his charge, and then paid his fine, the NBA's own internal investigation revealed that the coach was telling the truth. Javie, a born referee (his father was an NFL official and his grandfather umpired in the American League), was, in his own words, taking "absolute delight" in Riley's misfortunes and openly rooting against the Heat during a game in which he was working. And in all of its infinite wisdom and commitment to fair play, the league determined—very quietly—that the penalty for vindictively petty officiating was a $1,000 slap on the wrist.

No apology or refund was ever offered to Riley.

COLLEGE BASKETBALL

Jayhawks Savings Time
March 21, 1986: Midwest Regional Semifinals, #1 Kansas vs. #5 Michigan State

It was revered visionary Benjamin Franklin who said, "Lost time is never found again." And in recognizing how this inability to control the clock would years later haunt American sports fans and erode their belief in the Almighty, Franklin added, "Beer is living proof that God loves us."

It's possible that the sage of the bifocal wasn't prophesying the coming connection between sports fans, clock operators, and the need to forget our misfortunes inside the foam of a frosty mug. But he was really smart, and according to some narrowly circulated history books, quite the basketball fan.

In March of 1986—some 236 years after Franklin discovered electricity while installing an iron basketball goal on his driveway— time was truly lost, as was a Sweet 16 win for Michigan State.

In the Midwest Regional Semifinals (back in the salad days prior to the NCAA's nonsensical pod system) the road to the Final Four for the top-seeded Kansas Jayhawks ran through KU's home away from home, Kansas City's Kemper Arena, the site of their National Championship win two years later. But even though the fourth-seeded Michigan State Spartans were essentially playing a road game, it was the Spartans who held the lead down the stretch.

With 2:21 remaining in regulation, the Spartans went up by 4. But a number of seconds later, and after several passes by the Jayhawks set up a Ron Kellogg answer, the time read 2:20. No one noticed that the clock wasn't moving, or at least no one said anything—except Spartan head coach Jud Heathcote, who had left the bench and was desperately pounding on the table in front of NCAA tournament committee member Dave Hart, hoping to get someone's attention.

Approximately 10 seconds elapsed in the time it took the clock to record one tick. But clock operator Larry Bates was oblivious to the malfunction, and therefore he didn't alert the game officials that there was a problem, a requirement to correct the error. And according to a postgame explanation by Dick Shultz, another tournament committee member, "Time cannot be added or subtracted from the clock unless the amount of time gained or lost is precisely known by the officials or the clock operator."

Precision was clearly not the order of the day, and unfortunately for the Spartans, the amount of extra time left on the clock happened to be just enough for Kansas to mount a comeback. The Jayhawks made up a 6-point deficit in the final minute of play, sending the contest to overtime with a last-second game-tying basket.

"If those 10 seconds go off the clock like they should have," observed the agitated Heathcote, "the game would have been over before [Kansas] tied it."

Would have, could have, should have . . . but wasn't.

KU rolled over the Spartans in the extra five minutes of play, advancing to the Elite Eight with a 96-86 definitive "last-second" win, and eventually landing in the hallowed grounds of the Final Four.

Time and Time Again

March 23, 1990: Southeast Regional Semifinals,
#1 Michigan State vs. #4 Georgia Tech

Steve Smith had replaced Scott Skiles as the team's leader, the location for their Sweet 16 appearance had moved from Kansas City to New Orleans, and Michigan State was now a top seed. But unfortunately the Spartans' NCAA Tournament fortunes hadn't changed much in four years. Fate and the game clock were still squarely against them.

Up by 2 points with 5 seconds to play, eventual two-time All-American Steve Smith went to the free throw line with a chance to seal the deal for the Spartans and send them to the Elite 8. But the man who would leave the Spartans a year later as their all-time leading scorer missed the front end of the one-and-one, and it was rebounded by Georgia Tech's Dennis Scott.

With the final seconds slipping away, Scott made a quick pass to fellow future NBA star Kenny Anderson, who, already on a dead sprint, raced the ball up the floor and released a shot from the 3-point arc just as the clock was expiring. The shot was good, the refs awarded a 3-pointer, and a Tournament-advancing celebration commenced among the Yellow Jackets.

It was the kind of incredible final-shot moment that we only get from NCAA Tournament basketball. But three minutes later, after the officials had gathered at the scoring table to discuss if in fact Anderson's shot had been a 3-pointer, and finally decided that it had not, the disappointment for Georgia Tech was striking, the kind of letdown that we also only get from NCAA Tournament basketball.

Instead of a for-the-ages Georgia Tech win, everyone was headed to overtime.

Spartans coach Jud Heathcote, however, was still not happy, and not because his team let one slip away in the closing seconds. The referees had conferred, and rightly so, to make sure that the game-deciding decision about the location of Anderson's foot was correct. But the placement of his foot was in reality a moot point. Anderson's heroic game-tying runner came after the buzzer had sounded and the clock read zeros, and the officials who were instead focused on his feet should have waved it off.

"You've got an awful lot at stake here, for them, for the schools, for the conferences," Heathcote said. "There should not be a mistake by the officials on whether a shot beat the buzzer or didn't beat the buzzer."

The mistake, though, was made. And it was enough to rob Michigan State of a second Sweet 16 win in four years. The Spartans lost 81-80 in overtime when Dennis Scott banked home a jumper with just eight seconds left.

Minnesota coach Clem Haskins, whose Gophers were preparing to play Tech two days later in the Regional Final, agreed with Heathcote about the need for replay, saying, "There's too much at stake if a guy misses a call, if we let a clock determine a game."

But predictably, Tech coach Bobby Cremmins didn't agree with his two colleagues. "Kenny's shot was on the borderline, no doubt about it. But good officials have got to let it go. When it's that close, it's got to count."

Unless you just happen to be on the short of end of "close." That's when you'd like "good officials" to get the call right.

Scoreboard

March 6, 1975: ACC Tournament 1st Round,
North Carolina vs. Wake Forest

There are some places in this country where one aspect of life, and specifically a certain sport, transcends the rest of existence. In Texas it's high school football. On the frozen lakes of Minnesota, hockey will always be king. And along the green hills and small towns that dot the stretch of North Carolina known as Tobacco Road, it's a craze for college basketball.

The rivalry of the four schools on Tobacco Road, born by a triangular twenty-five-mile proximity to each other, includes Duke, North Carolina, North Carolina State, and Wake Forest (now about a hundred miles west after moving to Winston-Salem in 1956). And over the years it has provided some of the best and biggest games in college basketball history.

Few are as memorable, or controversial, as the 1975 ACC Tournament meeting between the North Carolina Tar Heels and the Wake Forest Demon Deacons. For the Tar Heels, this classic game has lived on as an incredible comeback that eventually led to an overtime win, accompanied two days later by an ACC Tournament championship. For the Demon Deacons, the injustice of the day is still palpable more than three decades later.

The meeting between the two teams was a random occurrence decided by a fickle flip of a coin. North Carolina finished the ACC's regular season in a three-way tie for second place, and was given the privilege of playing the fading Demon Deacons (2-10 in conference) by a coin toss. It was a stroke of good luck that quickly turned sour once the game began.

From the beginning, Wake gave Carolina more than it could handle, matching the superior Heels throughout, and besting them at the end to the tune of an 8-point lead with just 50 seconds to play. But the tide turned when a Phil Ford jumper reduced that deficit to 6 and a Mitch Kupchak layup a few seconds later pulled the Heels to within 4.

The floodgates were bowing, but not bursting, and Wake Forest was still in great shape, inbounding the ball with 34 seconds left and now clinging to a 90-86 lead. But as the long pass by Jerry Schellenberg made its way down court to Skip Brown, the referees blew the whistle and breached the dam. They said that Schellenberg's pass had grazed the underside of the low-hanging scoreboard and the ball was now out of bounds to the Tar Heels.

The Deacons' spirited protests of the call fell on deaf ears, and play resumed with Carolina in improper possession of the ball under the Wake basket, a position that allowed them to get a quick pass into Walter Davis, who with 24 seconds left made it a 2-point game. A missed Demon Deacon free throw later, the flood was official, and with just two ticks left on the clock Brad Hoffman sent the game to overtime tied at 90-90.

With the aid of the referee's life preserver, North Carolina successfully navigated Wake's waters to the 101-100 overtime win, eventually earning a spot in the NCAA Tournament's Sweet 16.

And to this day, many Wake Forest fans still feel the pangs of injustice when they hear the word *scoreboard*.

Vandy's Vitiated Victory

March 21, 2004: NCAA Tournament 2nd Round,
#3 North Carolina State vs. #6 Vanderbilt

"A little madness in the spring is wholesome," wrote Emily Dickinson, in what we can only assume was a poem inspired by her initial impressions of a college basketball game. And later when she wrote, "I can wade grief, whole pools of it," she was no doubt moved by the poignant agonies of the North Carolina State Wolfpack in 2004.

If ever there was a representation of March Madness worthy of storage in a time capsule so that future worlds could understand this strange affliction that debilitates mankind by the millions each spring, it was the 2004 Tournament matchup between North Carolina State and Vanderbilt. Wolfpack junior Julius Hodge, the ACC's player of the year in 2004, captured the spirit of its ending with five pointed words: "I cannot believe we lost."

With 3:45 left to play and N.C. State up by 11, the fans in Raleigh were making plans for a trip to the Sweet 16—a place they hadn't traveled to since 1989. But Vanderbilt, no Tournament slouch, had other ideas.

The Commodores' rally was jump-started when the Wolfpack fouled Matt Freije during a 3-point attempt, not once, but twice. Freije, who finished with a game-high 31 points, made all six free throws. But perhaps even more importantly, the second of the two fouls had been the fifth on Hodge, leaving the Wolfpack without its best player for the final two minutes.

The wheels were shimmying on the Wolfpack's car, but they had yet to officially come off . . . until, with 1:51 to go and State still up by 6, Vandy's Scott Hundley came up with a steal and then passed it ahead to teammate Corey Smith, who sprinted toward the basket. Trying to catch Smith from behind was Wolfpack forward Marcus Melvin, but as he reached Smith and attempted to get into a defensive position, Melvin stumbled and fell, and both players hit the floor in a tangling of feet.

By all accounts from the eyes that saw it, Melvin's takedown of Smith was an unfortunate accident brought on by the speed and energy of athleticism. Most also agreed, however, that it should have been called a foul, which it was. But when referee David Libbey blew his whistle to dole out the discipline, he called Melvin for a spirit-crushing intentional foul.

With the impassioned protests of the Wolfpack bench providing the underlying soundtrack, Smith made both free throws. Then on the ensuing possession—awarded because of

Libbey's prohibitively punitive penalty—Vandy's Mario Moore completed the 5-point play with a 3-pointer from twenty-five feet.

Certainly the players of North Carolina State bear much of the blame for their eventual 75-73 loss to Vanderbilt. The Commodores scored an eye-popping 21 points in their final seven possessions (do the math), with 9 of those points coming from the free-throw line. And Vanderbilt, for sure, deserves much of the credit. They didn't miss a single foul shot in the second half (13-13), and in the closing minute of play they picked up two huge defensive rebounds.

But to be truthful—because in the words of the inimitable Ms. Dickinson, "Shame need not crouch"—the biggest play of the game, by far, was the five-point present proffered by Libbey.

Traveling the Road to the Final Four

March 25, 2005: Syracuse Regional Semifinals,
#1 North Carolina vs. #5 Villanova

To hear the giants of basketball tell it, Roy Williams is one of the greatest coaches in basketball history.

Fellow head coach and former Tar Heel Larry Brown said of Williams, "He's as good a coach as our sport has."

Michael Jordan, who played at North Carolina when Williams was an assistant coach under Dean Smith, said, "I truly learned a lot from Coach Williams. I consider Roy not only to be a great coach, but a good friend."

And NBA Hall of Fame player and TV analyst Bill Walton said, "Roy Williams is one of the select few of the greatest coaches in the entire game of basketball. Coach Williams's impact on young people's lives throughout this great land will change the course of history."

If we ignore Walton's well-known love of uncontained hyperbole,

March 25, 2005, Villanova vs. North Carolina: Villanova's Allan Ray is in disbelief after he's called for traveling by referee Tom O'Neill.

the praise for Williams is consistent. He's great, even though until he finally captured his first National Championship at North Carolina in 2005, after seventeen years as a head coach, the media largely labeled him an underachiever who couldn't win the big one.

With humble apologies to the coach, the disrespect continues with our suggestion that without a very helpful official's assist in the Sweet 16, his championship cupboard might still be bare.

The top-seeded Tar Heels entered the Tournament sputtering a bit, having lost to Georgia Tech 78-75 in the semifinals of the ACC Tournament. But that loss was quickly put behind North Carolina with two easy wins to begin the NCAAs, a 28-point rout of Oakland (Michigan), and a 27-point thumping of Iowa State. The good times continued in the Sweet 16 against Villanova, with Carolina having survived a good first half by the Wildcats to take an 11-point lead with 4:49 to play.

But that's when Villanova began to mount a comeback. With North Carolina's lead at ten and the clock reading 3:45, the Wildcats defense held North Carolina scoreless for the next three minutes, shrinking their deficit to as low as two in the process. After a back-and-forth exchange of free throws lifted the Tar Heel lead to three, Villanova's Allan Ray drove to the hoop, made the basket, and appeared to draw a foul that would have sent him to the line with an "and-1" chance to tie the game. Just nine seconds remained.

"I thought the ref called a foul," Ray said.

"I thought we had a 3-point play," added Villanova coach Jay Wright.

Referee Tom O'Neill blew the whistle to make the call, but instead of calling the foul, counting the basket, and giving Ray a free throw to try to tie the game—as everyone not wearing Tar Heel blue expected—O'Neill whistled Ray for traveling. There was no foul, no basket, and by virtue of those negatives, no more chance for Villanova, who eventually fell short in their upset bid, 67-66.

"Once they called traveling, I felt like a kid in a candy store," said North Carolina's Melvin Scott. "I was so happy."

The outraged Villanova fans, however, were not, taking O'Neill's season-ending call as a cue to litter the court with plastic bottles in protest.

After the game a very diplomatic Roy Williams told reporters, "We feel as fortunate as we can possibly feel. Those were some pretty hairy moments there at the end."

Every bit as hairy as the monkey that was removed from his back ten days later in St. Louis, when he and his Heels cut down the nets at the Final Four.

Give Him a T . . . and CPR

January 21, 2006: Houston at UAB

> **Prat·fall** - *n.* - A fall on the buttocks.
> *The American Heritage Dictionary*
> *of the English Language*

Longtime college basketball coach Tom Penders was quite the athlete in his younger days. Along with leading the UConn basketball team to the NCAA Tournament twice as their captain and point guard (1965 and 1967), he captained the Huskies baseball team to the College World Series (1965), making him one of the few players to participate in both NCAA championship tournament showcases.

He played a season in the Cleveland Indians farm system. He was a five-time national champion in fast-pitch softball. In 2001 the UConn athletic department gave Penders the Red O'Neill Award for Lifetime Achievement. And the *Hartford Courant* named him one of the three greatest athletes to come from the town of Stratford, Connecticut.

Tom Penders is clearly a man of many skills and no doubt still athletic enough, now in his 60s, to avoid the occasional pratfall. One should think.

Penders's Houston Cougars were on the road to take on the Blazers of Alabama–Birmingham in an otherwise typical regular-season Conference USA game. And through the first 19 minutes of the first half, the game was typical, and played without a noteworthy incident. But that all changed when, with only 52 seconds remaining before halftime and following a borderline foul on Houston's Oliver Lafayette, the game took a second-to-none turn to the absurd.

As referee John Hampton went to the scorer's table to call and record the foul on Lafayette, Penders, mildly displeased with the call, suddenly dropped to the floor. Noticing the hollow thud that came from his left, Hampton turned to Penders—now lying flat on the hardwood—and promptly whistled him for a technical foul, convinced that the "pratfall" by the coach was done to show him up.

A few seconds went by . . . and nothing. Penders wasn't arguing, complaining, or . . . moving.

The paramedics on hand were quick to Penders's aid, treating the coach with oxygen, and eventually carrying him from the floor on a stretcher to the prayers and well wishes of the hushed partisan crowd.

It quickly became obvious that Penders's collapse to the floor was not a demonstrative protest of Hampton's foul call on Lafayette. The sixty-year-old Penders was diagnosed with cardiomyopathy, a stiffening inflammation of the heart muscle, in 1991, and in 1997 he had a pacemaker implanted to regulate and control the very livable but often very serious condition. But because of the weakness in the muscle, he occasionally experiences faintness.

It's probably safe to assume that John Hampton didn't know about Penders's heart. So his spur-of-the-moment assessment of a technical is forgivable in light of his ignorance about Penders's medical history. But where the pardons end, and what will forever taint Hampton, who by all accounts is a solid basketball official, was his refusal to rescind the technical foul when it became clear that it was not disrespect but a lack of oxygen to the brain that took Penders to the floor.

That's right, Penders was still given the technical foul, and UAB was still awarded two free throws, which they made.

Penders, who recovered enough to return to the bench in the second half, joked with reporters after the game, "It's a good thing I didn't die. They would have gotten two more free throws and possession [of the ball]."

Conference USA Assistant Commissioner Chris Woolard

sided with the coach, but couldn't have been more vanilla in his condemnation, saying in a statement, "It appears that the crew exercised poor judgment."

Poor judgment is chasing a heavy bean meal with four cups of coffee shortly before boarding an international flight. Poor judgment is letting Rick Salomon (of Paris Hilton videography fame) date your daughter. Or Joe Francis (creator of "Girls Gone Wild"). Or Mike Tyson.

Referee John Hampton wasn't guilty of "poor judgment." He made one of the most astonishingly asinine judgments in the history of sports.

Bad Shave

Summer 2007: The United States vs. Tim Donaghy

It was Agatha Christie who said, "Where large sums of money are concerned, it is advisable to trust nobody."

And it was former Speaker of the House Newt Gingrich who said, "You can't trust anybody with power."

The mystery writer and lifetime politician were probably addressing the potential pitfalls that the sports world will forever face; most specifically, the danger that lies within the "large sums of money" world of Las Vegas and the powerful people who control its sportsbooks.

And the people with the power to affect final scores.

In basketball, point-shaving has a long and shameful history, with perhaps its most infamous case involving the indictments that were handed down in 1951 to players from four New York area colleges: City College, Manhattan College, New York University, and Long Island University. Before it was all said and done seven different schools, including Kentucky, and 32 players were implicated.

In the mix of indictments, but spared a felony charge because New York State had no relevant statute regarding referees and bribery, was NBA referee Sol Levy. He was paid $1,000 prior to each game in question (he was accused of fixing six games, but only convicted for three), and assuming that he came through for the gamblers by getting key players to foul out early, he'd get the rest of his money afterward.

This was 1951. There was no ESPN, no 24-hour sports talk radio, and the NBA was barely a blip on the nation's radar when compared to its love affair with the college game. So Sol Levy avoided widespread condemnation, and any long-term infamy was swallowed up by Adolf Rupp's Kentucky Wildcats when they were suspended by the NCAA for the 1952–53 season.

But imagine if you will, if the same thing were to happen today. The NBA is huge and sports information is omnipresent. Would the Sol Levys of the world survive the contempt of today?

Thanks to Tim "Trading Dignity for Dollars" Donaghy, we don't have to imagine. In 2007 the 13-year referee pleaded guilty to two felonies—conspiracy to commit wire fraud and conspiracy to transmit gambling information across state lines—for accepting bribes from gamblers and gambling himself on games that he was officiating.

It seems that the $260,000 he was making annually as an NBA referee wasn't enough.

We may never know the full extent of Donaghy's treachery to the league and its fans. But what we do know is that he used his position to change the outcome of several games. Two playoff games involving the Phoenix Suns have drawn the most suspicion.

According to Stats LLC, and reported by the *New York Post*, during the 2006–2007 season Donaghy led all referees with 177 technical fouls called—20 more than the next highest ref. He was also second in the league for fouling players out of games, and had the third most awarded free throws. All effective ways in swinging the final score a good three to five points.

But when looking at Donaghy with a gambler's eye, his impact is even clearer. Sports gambling expert R. J. Bell examined Donaghy's game history and found that during one ten-game stretch of games worked by Donaghy in 2007 the point spread moved more than 1½ points before tip-off, a sure sign that big money was being placed on one specific team. And according to Bell, in all ten instances the big money bet ended up as winning money paid out.

And during the final two years of his tarnished career, when the FBI was investigating, Donaghy's games beat the over/under 57% of the time—as compared to just 44% the previous two seasons. Bell says the odds of that swing in offense happening randomly are one in 1000.

The NBA will survive this, of course. Loyal fans aren't going to turn away from the league because its referees are tarnished. The players have been sullying up the league for years without consequence, so why should anything change because of the officials?

The only one who may not survive this is Donaghy himself. The FBI first got wind of the gambling scheme during its investigation into the Gambino crime family. And as compared to the NBA, that's probably not an association you'd want to be involved with.

I wanted to have a career in sports when I was young, but I had to give it up. I'm only six feet tall, so I couldn't play basketball. I'm only 190 pounds so I couldn't play football. And I have 20-20 vision, so I couldn't be a referee.

—JAY LENO
COMEDIAN

I think you enjoy the game more if you don't know the rules. Anyway, you're on the same wavelength as the referee.

—JONATHAN DAVIES
FORMER RUGBY PLAYER

Get used to the phrase: How could both referees have missed that?

—MIKE BROPHY OF *The Hockey News*
WHEN THE NHL ADOPTED ITS
TWO-REFEREE SYSTEM IN 1998

HOCKEY

There is an in-house Canadian controversy as to the exact origins of ice hockey. Montreal has long been credited as the birthplace of the sport, but both Kingston, Ontario, and Windsor, Nova Scotia, also lay claim to that honor. But not to be the bearers of bad news, or the grinches that stole Canuck national pride and the glory of the Maple Leaf, but credit for the Canadian national pastime actually lies 3,500 miles away in The Netherlands.

Several sixteenth-century Dutch paintings show a group of frolicking townspeople playing a hockey-like sport on one of Holland's many frozen canals. And we know for a fact that British soldiers fighting in what would later become Canada didn't combine field hockey with the native sport of lacrosse and then introduce that hybrid to wintry ice-covered ponds until the eighteenth century.

So along with wooden shoes, windmills, the world's first navigable submarine, and a visionary wrinkle on dating that has saved thrifty men everywhere countless millions of dollars, the Dutch deserve our many thanks for hockey.

But certainly Canada gets honorable-mention recognition for

the game's first official rulebook, all major innovations over the past two hundred years, and Billy Coutu, the first player to be suspended from the NHL for life after he punched out referee Jerry LaFlamme during a brawl at the end of Game 4 of the 1927 Stanley Cup Finals—an act that many players since have had good reason to envy.

Gifting The Great One

May 27, 1993: Campbell Conference Finals Game 6, Maple Leafs at Kings

Wayne Gretzky, like Michael Jordan, Babe Ruth, Johnny Unitas, and Muhammad Ali, will always be an iconic cut above the rest. Gretzky is the man all future great goal scorers will be compared to. His number 99 stands out as perhaps the most recognizable jersey in the history of team sports. And his singular impact on the landscape of hockey runs deeper and more far-reaching than anyone who has ever laced up skates, put on cleats, or personalized a sneaker.

It was Gretzky's days in Los Angeles, punctuated by the Kings' Stanley Cup Finals run in 1993, that made hockey a popular Sunbelt sport, setting the stage for NHL franchises in Anaheim, San Jose, Phoenix, Miami, Tampa Bay, Atlanta, and Dallas. That's the power of The Great One. Or in the mind's eye of Toronto Maple Leafs fans, the impact of an infamous non-call by referee Kerry Fraser.

It's hard not to transfer some of the residual sympathy we feel for Cubs fans over to the diehards who bleed blue for the Leafs. Like the Cubs, the Leafs have been around since the early days of their sport. They boast some of hockey's all-time greatest names, including Conn Smythe and Terry Sawchuck. And at one point, Toronto's success on the ice was unmatched, winning a total of eighteen Stanley Cups, including an impressive run in the 1960s of four cups in six years, ending in 1967.

The Leafs were the toast of hockey, the envy of their peers, and the lords of Lord Stanley's Cup.

But then . . . deafening silence followed. Pins dropped, and were heard. Crickets chirped. The raucous joy in Leafville was no more.

Since 1967, and coincidentally since the NHL expanded from beyond its original six teams, Toronto hasn't lifted another Cup. In fact, in the four decades since their last championship, the Leafs haven't even been within sight of the Cup, failing to make it past the semifinals the five times they made it that far. The closest, and cruelest, of those playoff near misses came in 1993 at the hands of Gretzky and Fraser.

It was Game 6 of the Campbell Conference Finals, Toronto led the series 3-2, and just before overtime began in a 4-4 tie game, Toronto went down a man on a questionable boarding call against Glen Anderson. Not questionable because it wasn't a penalty, or shouldn't always be called in the first or second periods. But this was the closing minute of a game headed to overtime when NHL officials are almost always whistle swallowers—as they were moments later.

On the power play, and now in the first minute of sudden death, all eyes were on Gretzky. And one would then assume that all eyes saw Gretzky's stick come up high during an exchange and whack Doug Gilmour across the nose. A whack that sent Gilmour off the ice to get stitches for his busted sniffer, and one that should have sent Gretzky to the penalty box for an automatic five-minute penalty.

Maybe referee Kerry Fraser missed the hit, and the subsequent blood that followed. Or maybe he was afraid to send hockey's god off the ice in the deciding moments of the conference finals and risk the wrath of new commissioner Gary Bettman, at that time less than four months on the job. But what we do know is that Fraser didn't call the penalty that the high stick warranted. And while Gilmour was on the bench getting stitches for his nose, Gretzky scored the game-winning goal.

The result of Fraser's non-call was an L.A. victory and a Game 7 back in Toronto, which the Kings would win 5-4 on the shoulders of a Gretzky hat trick—a game Gretzky would later call one of the best he ever played.

Ten years after Fraser helped continue Toronto's Cup-less suffering with his gift to Gretzky, and on the night he refereed his 1,500th career NHL game, the much-maligned official admitted to missing the call in '93, calling it "unfortunate."

Kerry Fraser Redux

May 25, 1998: Eastern Conference Finals Game 2, Sabres at Capitals

Five years after he made ordering food from restaurants in Toronto that employ bitter hockey fans in the kitchen an iffy proposition, Kerry Fraser took Buffalo off his list of pleasant vacation destinations. Not that he's feeling the yearly pang of loss each Labor Day weekend when the National Buffalo Wing Festival crowns its "Wing King." Get your tickets now.

In the second season of life inside the new Marine Midland Arena (later changed to HSBC Arena), and a year after winning their first division title in sixteen years, the Buffalo Sabres made their deepest trek into the playoffs in eighteen years. After dominating the Flyers 4 games to 1 in the opening round and routing Montreal in a 4-0 sweep in the conference semifinals, the Sabres found themselves facing off with Washington just one step away from playing for the Cup. And with the recent Olympic gold-medal winner Dominik Hasek in goal (that year he also became the first goalie to win the Hart Trophy twice), no one was betting against Buffalo.

The Dominator easily held serve in Game 1 of the Eastern Conference Finals, with Buffalo winning 2-0. And through the first period and a half of Game 2, Hasek continued to hold the Capitals scoreless. But with Buffalo clinging to a 1-0 lead,

Washington's Peter Bondra finally broke the drought with a goal from in front of the net. A game-tying goal that in reality should have been disallowed because Bondra's skate was in the crease.

No one is faulting Kerry Fraser for missing the call. When bodies and sticks are flying at the speed of hockey, you could miss a severed head in the crease. Mistakes happen all the time. Which is exactly the reason the league has instant replay. Of course, it only works when it's consulted, which in this case it wasn't, and why Fraser deservedly gets the blame.

Now fast-forward the action to sudden-death overtime, with the score knotted up 2-2 (although Washington had scored only one legitimate goal). Clearing the puck from his end by the Caps' Esa Tikkanen should have resulted in an easy icing call and a face-off in the Washington zone. But Fraser and his linesman swallowed their whistles again. After Sabres defenseman Jason Wooley touched the puck (icing), Caps winger Todd Krygier was able to secure it in front of the Sabres' net and beat Hasek for the controversial game-winning score.

The next day Bryan Lewis, the NHL's director of officiating, told *The Buffalo News* regarding the overtime mistake, "Obviously there was an error on our part. The bottom line was that there was a judgment call by an official on a split-second play. We could have done it a little better."

As for the non-call for video replay on Washington's first goal by Bondra, that was "at the referee's discretion."

Mistakes and mistaken discretion cost the Sabres the opportunity to take a luxurious 2-0 series lead with the best-of-seven conference finals shifting back home to Buffalo. Instead, Washington tied the series, won the next two, and eventually bumped off Buffalo in six.

The Capitals went on to play the Red Wings in the Stanley Cup Finals. The Sabres got an official NHL apology.

Creased Cup

June 19, 1999: Stanley Cup Finals Game 6, Stars at Sabres

Speaking of the Sabres, important playoff games, skates in the crease, and the failure of instant replay, welcome to the most controversial finish to a Stanley Cup Finals, ever.

Those of you still awake when Game 6 of the 1999 Finals went to a third overtime in the wee hours of the East Coast morning remember the scene. The Sabres and the Dallas Stars were nearing the end of what amounted to an exhausting double-header of hockey. Not only were the players no longer hitting each other or skating to the offensive end with any speed—only eleven combined shots were attempted in the final overtime—they were barely still standing. Following the marathon, the Stars' Mike Modano admitted to having a "clean break" in his left wrist for the final three games, while teammate Brett Hull confessed to playing the end of the series with a pair of groin pulls and a severely damaged left knee.

Ironically, if Hull hadn't been able to continue, the game would have most likely ended without controversy or recognition.

Nearly 55 minutes into overtime (22 seconds short of setting the record for the longest game ever played), it was Hull who scored the Cup-clinching goal, ending the torturous battle and beginning years of divided debate. Hull's skate was shown to be in the crease when he recovered his own missed shot and finally forced the puck past a prone Dominik Hasek. And as we all knew in '99 because of its controversial implementation in several games of consequence, the rules stated that an offensive player's skate in the crease prior to the arrival of the puck automatically made the goal illegal.

The NHL said that they did in fact review the replay of Hull's goal, but there was no violation. And in no way were they dissuaded from overturning the score and continuing the game

Game 6, 1999 Stanley Cup Finals: Brett Hull's skate is clearly in the crease as he scores the Cup-winning goal against Dominik Hasek.

because of the jubilant celebration on the ice that had commenced among the Stars and their supporters. But the Sabres saw the replay, the fans in the arena saw the replay, the night-owl hockey fans across North America saw the replay, and the NHL's claim of a review on the up-and-up simply didn't wash.

Sabres coach Lindy Ruff told reporters that he'd sought out commissioner Gary Bettman after the game to demand an explanation, but "[Bettman] turned his back on me. He almost looked to me like he knew this might be a tainted goal and there was no answer for it."

Sabres forward Joe Juneau called the NHL "gutless," and said, "Everybody will remember this as the Stanley Cup that was never won."

And a bewildered Hasek quipped to the press, "I don't understand what the video judge is doing. Maybe he was in the bathroom. Maybe he was sleeping. Maybe he doesn't know the rule."

Maybe Hasek was right.

According to NHL director of officiating Bryan Lewis—who reviewed the goal with two video replay officials—Hull was permitted to be in the crease because he maintained control and possession of the puck.

"A puck that rebounds off the goalie, the goal post, or an opposing player is not deemed to be a change of possession," said Lewis. "Therefore, Hull would be deemed to be in control of the puck and allowed to shoot and score a goal, even though the one foot would be in the crease in advance of the puck."

But the NHL rulebook for the 1998–99 season did not mention anything about "control of the puck" when interpreting the crease rule (added in 1991 to help protect goalies), and in fact the violation had been applied rather liberally throughout the regular season and playoffs, stipulating that the puck always had to proceed a player into the crease.

Two days later commissioner Gary Bettman announced that the crease rule would change for the upcoming season to a "no harm, no foul" policy that specified an attacking player's position does not in itself determine a violation of the rule. He also added that "crease judgments" would exclusively be in the hands of the on-ice referees, and no longer subject to video review.

Which was all well and good for the 1999–2000 NHL season, but in no way did it explain why the existing rules and standards weren't applied to Brett Hull that June morning in Buffalo.

And that explains why a great Stanley Cup Final will forever be tainted.

A Goal From All Angles

April 15, 2000: Eastern Conference Quarterfinals Game 2,
Sabres at Flyers

It's not that we want to pick on the Sabres. Life has done that enough, with their arena's ice-crashing $4 million Jumbotron scoreboard (just two months after it opened, and just hours before a game was to begin); their indicted former owner, John Rigas of Adelphia Communications bank, wire and securities fraud fame; and of course the team's bankruptcy that resulted from Rigas's reign. It's just that along with those adversities, they've also been subjected to a progressive string of blind goal judges.

Add the many Sabres stumbles to the Bills Super Bowl futility, the city's ninety-three inches of annual snowfall, and consensus preference among honeymooners for the Canadian side of Niagara Falls, and you have to wonder if Buffalo's century of plight is searing karmic retribution fomented by the ghost of President William McKinley, the municipality's most famous murder victim.

Another explanation could be simple bad luck coupled with a series of bad referees. We won't pass judgment on either assertion.

Down to the top-seeded Flyers by a game in the first round of the playoffs, the Sabres were in desperate need of a break if they were going to steal one on the road. They were less than a year removed from Game 6 of the Stanley Cup Finals and Brett Hull's skate in the crease, but the Sabres team playing in 2000 was miles away from the club that came so close to the Cup. Joe Juneau was gone to Ottawa, an injured groin limited Dominik Hasek to just thirty-five games, and Buffalo squeaked into the playoffs as the eighth and final seed.

Buffalo was up a goal in the second period and trying to kill a penalty when the break they so desperately needed ended up being a heart-breaking back-breaker. Philadelphia's John LeClair fired a hard slap shot that managed to get past the left side of Hasek for the game-tying power-play goal. But the shot was so hard it wasn't exactly clear how the puck got past Hasek, who appeared to have that side of the goal covered.

The answer: It didn't get past Hasek. It went around him, getting into the goal through the side of the net.

"It was a 99-mph, 100-mph shot," Hasek said. "I looked at it right away and blamed myself. I thought maybe I made a mistake."

The mistake was not Hasek's, but the NHL's. The video replay official on hand, Mike Condon, immediately reviewed the goal, as he should have. But for a reason that still remains unclear all these years later, he didn't have access to the crucial angle (supplied by ESPN's "Net Cam") that showed the puck entering the goal outside the left post. The two angles Condon saw were both inconclusive.

Six minutes after the goal was scored, the new and definitive angle came to light when someone knocked on the NHL officials' box and told them that ESPN was showing that the puck entered through the net. But by then play had resumed and it was too late for Buffalo.

In the words of conciliatory NHL supervisor John D'Amico, doing damage control at the arena, "We can't review what we can't see."

Following the game, an eventual 2-1 Philadelphia win that led to a 4-1 series triumph, Flyers coach Craig Ramsay said, "I have seen it all."

Sabres forward Dixon Ward called the missed replay "embarrassing," and said, "A great hockey game has to be marred by something stupid again."

A stunned and bitter Miroslav Satan said, "Everybody in this dressing room feels like the NHL owes us something."

And NHL Executive Vice President and Director of Hockey Operations Colin Campbell made the highly unusual move of addressing the controversy by calling into the Sabres postgame show on the Empire Sports Network, saying, "You think we wanted this to happen. It's the last thing you want to happen. You want a game to end because one team played better than the other. Every Buffalo fan should be upset."

After getting hosed twice in ten months, you can be sure that every Buffalo fan was.

The Flyers and Leon Stickle

May 24, 1980: Stanley Cup Finals Game 6, Flyers at Islanders

For each and every sports franchise there is at least one name that angers and enrages embittered fans at its mere mention. And years, decades, and generations later that seething anger remains at the surface, ready to blow with just two little words. For Boston Red Sox fans, those words are Bill Buckner. If you're a Portland Trail Blazers fan, it's Sam Bowie—the ill-famed center from Kentucky picked one spot *ahead* of Michael Jordan in the 1984 NBA draft. And for the Philadelphia Flyers, it's Leon Stickle.

Most people know Philadelphia fans as the miscreants who booed and pelted Santa Claus with snowballs at halftime of a 1968 Eagles game, cheered the serious neck injury in 1999 that led the Cowboys' Michael Irvin to retire, and threw batteries at J. D. Drew two years after he jilted the Phillies. A bunch of sad sacks who celebrate fictional boxer Rocky Balboa with a statue (none exists for real-life champion Joe Frazier), and a group so desperate for any victory parade that they once focused their championship dreams on local horse Smarty Jones. When the three-year-old previously undefeated colt missed taking the Triple Crown because of a loss in the Belmont Stakes, Philly fans were inconsolable.

But before these fans began muting the pain of "The Philly Curse" at the bars and clubs on South Street, there was 1980, the year the Eagles won their first NFC Championship, the Phillies won their first World Series, the 76ers played in the NBA Finals, and the Flyers, who had a professional sports record-setting 35-game unbeaten streak during the regular season, did battle for Lord Stanley's Cup.

Not to mention that hometown virtuosos Daryl Hall and John Oates had just released chart-topper "Kiss on My List."

It was indeed a sublime time in the birthplace of American democracy.

With Game 6 of the Stanley Cup Finals knotted at 1 in the first period, and with the series favoring the New York Islanders 3 games to 2, Isles winger Clark Gillies took the puck into the offensive zone, dropped it back on a pass to center Butch Goring, who then fed it to Duane Sutter, who knocked home the tie-breaking goal for the 2-1 New York advantage. Nice movement of the puck to set up the goal, but with one big problem. When Gillies passed the puck back to Goring, it traveled across the blue line and back into neutral ice, leaving Gillies in the offensive end and illegally offsides.

It was an obvious call seen by almost everyone inside the Nassau Coliseum, except linesman Leon Stickle. Upon seeing the replay after the game Stickle, who twenty-three years later would become the NHL's supervisor of officials, said, "I guess I blew it. Maybe there was black tape on Goring's stick and it confused me."

The Islanders pushed their lead to 4-2 with a big second period. But the Flyers were able to battle back in third and tie it up 4-all, sending the game to overtime. However, their dreams of a comeback win on Long Island, and a very winnable Game 7 back in Philadelphia, ended when they got caught in a line change 7:11 into overtime and New York's Bobby Nystrom was able to score the Cup-winning goal.

The Islanders would go on to win four straight Stanley Cups to begin the 1980s. The Flyers haven't won a Cup since.

And for the diehard Philadelphians who populate Geno's Steaks twenty-four hours a day, the name Leon Stickle continues to live in infamy.

In-Flamed Canucks
April 15, 1989: Smythe Division Semifinals Game 7,
Canucks at Flames

Four hockey fans are mountain climbing together one afternoon, each climber a rabid fan of a different NHL team. One is from Ottawa, one is from Toronto, one from Calgary, and the final one from Vancouver.

As they climb higher and higher, the argument gets more and more heated as to which one of them is the most loyal fan. Finally, as they reach the summit, the climber from Ottawa takes an inspired running leap off the top of the mountain, yelling on the way down, "This is for the Senators!"

Not to be outdone, the climber from Toronto throws himself from the mountain, shouting, "This is for the Maple Leafs!"

Seeing these two climbers display their love and loyalty in such a profound way, the climber from Vancouver walks to the edge and yells, "This is for hockey fans everywhere!" He then pushes the fan from Calgary over the cliff.

It's an old hockey joke. And versatile, too. I'm sure if you've heard it told in Calgary, it's the Vancouver Canucks fan who takes the final plunge. Such is the relationship between these two very different cities that have one very big thing in common. A hatred for the other city's hockey team that is learned from the time each newly born fan is still in diapers. When it comes to this great hockey rivalry, hatred is pure, honorable, and a civic duty.

The source of the animosity between Vancouverites and Calgarians can be traced directly back to Game 7 of the first round of the 1989 playoffs, and Calgary's Joel Otto. At 6-foot-4, 220 pounds, Otto was an imposing figure on the ice. And with nearly two thousand penalty minutes in a career that lasted fourteen years, Otto was a powerful center who made the most of his dual roles as offensive weapon and physical force.

But it was his skate that turned out to be most damaging to the Vancouver Canucks.

In overtime of Game 7, heavily favored Calgary, the regular season's league leader with 117 points, was in grave danger of being upset by lowly Vancouver, a team that finished the year six games under .500. It would have been one of the great David-beats-Goliath moments in sports. It would have been . . . until a harmless shot by Jim Peplinski that was sure to be saved by Canucks goalie Kirk McLean was instead deflected past him by Otto's Goliath-sized skate.

Not wanting to trifle with minor issues such as an illegal goal scored by intentionally using a skate to redirect the puck, the officials ruled Otto's overtime goal good, ending the game and Vancouver's season, and building the foundation for a passionate rivalry that continues to burn with hatred today.

In 1994 the Canucks exacted a small measure of revenge with a double-overtime Game 7 win at Calgary that sent them on an eventual trip to the Stanley Cup Finals.

Ten years later the Flames returned the favor, winning their own first-round overtime Game 7 at Vancouver.

But in this long-running rivalry, nothing can compare to 1989 and the hockey injustice that will forever qualify the Flames' lone Stanley Cup as an odious offering by an erring official.

In a way an umpire is like a woman. He makes quick decisions, never reverses them, and doesn't think you're safe when you're out.

—LARRY GOETZ
NATIONAL LEAGUE UMPIRE (1935–1956)

There's no such thing as perfection. Mistakes happen. Officials are so hard on themselves. When they make a mistake, nobody feels worse than they do.

—JERRY MARKBREIT
NFL REFEREE (1976–1998)

The trouble with referees is that they just don't care which side wins.

—TOM CANTERBURY
FORMER COLLEGE BASKETBALL COACH

NATIONAL FOOTBALL LEAGUE

If baseball is America's national pastime, then the NFL is America's crazed passion.

Pro football was born on November 12, 1892, when William "Pudge" Heffelfinger was illegally paid $500 to lead the Allegheny Athletic Association football team over the Pittsburgh Athletic Club. Earning every penny paid that afternoon, it was Heffelfinger who picked up a Pittsburgh fumble and returned it 35 yards for the game-winning touchdown.

And now, more than a century later, the NFL pays over $3 billion annually in player salaries. Not too bad for a league that was originally formed during a meeting at a Hupmobile car dealership in Canton, Ohio, as a means of preventing other teams from stealing their players—and had to vote on its inaugural champion because too many of the competing teams had folded by mid-season.

Talk about your meager beginnings.

But despite today's wealth, the NFL remains the only professional league to employ part-time referees, many of whom spend their weekdays working as lawyers and doctors.

Which actually may be a good thing. Backgrounds in law and medicine would presumably make them better equipped to handle the aftermath of an off-field encounter with a wronged and intoxicated NFL fan.

The Tuck Rule

January 19, 2002: AFC Divisional Playoffs, Raiders at Patriots

Ask any Raiders fan what they think of the rule that robbed them of a playoff win at New England in 2002, and most will use a word that rhymes with "tuck." The formerly insignificant, now infamous "tuck rule," also known as NFL Rule 3, Section 21, Article 2, Note 2, reads: . . . *any intentional forward movement of [the passer's] arm starts a forward pass, even if the player loses possession of the ball as he is attempting to tuck it back toward his body.*

With less than 2 minutes remaining in the game and the Patriots trailing 13-10, the blitzing Charles Woodson knocked the ball from quarterback Tom Brady's hand. The Raiders recovered the fumble and seemingly sealed the victory. And even when the play went upstairs to be reviewed, the entire Oakland sideline was confident that they were going to sneak out of snowy New England with the win.

But when referee Walt Coleman came out from under the replay hood and signaled that it was instead an incomplete pass, giving possession back to New England, the Raiders bench was almost too stunned to argue.

Did Coleman make the right or wrong call? Or was he hamstrung by a badly written rule?

Forget for a moment the absurdity of a rule that results in an incompletion, yet at the same time acknowledges no pass attempt. Was it properly applied here? In Tom Brady's own words, the answer is no. Brady said, "I was throwing the ball. I was trying to get rid of the ball. I'm glad they ruled the way they did."

2002 Playoffs, Raiders at Patriots: Tom Brady's late-game fumble is wiped away by the NFL's now infamous "tuck rule."

But if in fact he was "throwing the ball," then the tuck rule doesn't apply. Therefore it's a fumble with 1:43 left in regulation, and the Raiders hold on to win by 3.

It's been described by head coach Mike Holmgren as the "50 Guys in a Bar Theory." The way it works is, if 50 guys in a bar think it's a fumble, then it's a fumble. And that night, certainly in every bar within a hundred miles of Northern California's East Bay, there were at least 50 guys crying fumble.

So with Brady's own admission that he wasn't tucking the ball, the replay that shows both of Brady's hands on the ball (reestablishing possession and ending any pass attempt), and Mike Holmgren's scientific formula of alehouse analysis, we have to conclude that it was a fumble.

And that means that the resulting replay reversal kept Oakland from going to Pittsburgh to play in the AFC Championship Game. It kept one of those two teams from playing the Rams in Super Bowl XXXVI. And it erroneously jump-started a Patriots dynasty that has placed Tom Brady and head coach Bill Belichick among the game's elite.

All of which means that in the NFL, there is no such thing as an insignificant rule.

Plundering the Pats
December 18, 1976: AFC Divisional Playoff, Patriots at Raiders

It was the Raiders vs. the Patriots in the playoffs, and there was a controversial play late in the game involving a hit on the quarterback. But this was the 1970s. No snow storm . . . no "tuck rule" . . . and no whiny Al Davis when all was said and done.

Not too unlike their namesake brethren from 200 years before, the 1976 Patriots threw off the yoke of oppression (ten years without a winning record, including a 3-11 mark in 1975) and declared their independence from the AFC East cellar with a bicentennial trip to the playoffs. It was the nation's biggest birthday; and to date, the Patriots' brightest year.

Facing off against the Raiders in Oakland, the league's best team with a 13-1 regular season record (the one loss coming at New England during a brutal stretch of five straight road games), no one gave the wildcard Patriots much of a chance. But that was a mistake. New England entered the playoffs on a six-game winning streak and boasted the league's second-ranked rushing offense (2,948 yards).

In the closing minute of play, and with the Patriots leading by 4, Ken Stabler and the Raiders faced a 3rd-and-18 from the New England 28. The entire stadium felt the situation's desperation.

Stabler dropped back to pass, looking long down the left sideline for running back Carl Garrett. But just then Ray "Sugar Bear" Hamilton broke free on a stunt, bearing down on Stabler and deflecting his arm as he threw the ball, and causing Oakland's third-down pass to fall harmlessly incomplete.

All eyes were focused on the bouncing ball downfield—and looking ahead to a next-to-impossible 4th-and-18 for Oakland—when they noticed that a flag had been thrown in the Raiders backfield near Stabler and Hamilton.

In a game that featured numerous uncalled cheap shots, including a George Atkinson tackle that broke the nose of New England tight end Russ Francis, referee Ben Dreith chose that moment—with less than 40 seconds to play—to call roughing the passer.

Instead of looking at 4th-and-18, and possibly their season, the Raiders got a gift first down at the New England 13-yard line. The understandably peeved-off Pats then put the ball even closer by drawing a pair of unsportsmanlike conduct penalties for continuing to argue the call.

With just 10 seconds remaining, Stabler snuck in from the 1, and the Raiders escaped The Coliseum with a skin-of-their teeth 24-21 win. Oakland then posted easy wins over Pittsburgh in the AFC Championship Game and Minnesota in Super Bowl XI, while the Patriots were left to ponder what might have been.

Mike Haynes, a Patriot at the time but a Raider later on, called the penalty on Hamilton "bogus." And Stabler himself said, "It wasn't a late hit."

But on the twenty-fifth anniversary of the play, Dreith stood by the call that made him public enemy #1 in Boston, telling the *Boston Globe*, "You bet. Roughing the passer."

Maybe by today's rules, which make having so much as cross words with a quarterback a 15-yard penalty, Dreith is right. But in 1976 it was still legal to hit a quarterback, almost all of the time.

The Immaculate Reception
December 23, 1972: AFC Divisional Playoffs, Raiders at Steelers

NFL Films dubbed the miracle catch and touchdown run by Steelers running back Franco Harris against the Raiders the "greatest play in NFL history." But for the millions of fans who've seen, debated, and marveled at the play that helped launch a dynasty, it's known as the "Immaculate Reception."

The Steelers would finish their 1970s decade of dominance with six Championship Game appearances and four Super Bowl titles. But heading into their December meeting with the Raiders in 1972, the franchise, dating all the way back to 1933, had never even won a playoff game. In fact, in the previous forty seasons they'd only made the postseason once, in 1947.

Which is why, when Ken Stabler scored on a 30-yard run with 1:13 remaining, giving the Raiders a 7-6 lead, Pittsburgh owner Art Rooney began to make his way to the Steelers locker room to congratulate his team on its best season to date—causing him to miss the controversial finish.

With 22 seconds left in the game, and the Steelers facing a desperation 4th-and-10 from their own 40, Terry Bradshaw dropped back to pass. And after escaping the pressure applied by defensive linemen Horace Jones and Tony Cline, he rifled a 25-yard pass down the middle of the field to running back Frenchy Fuqua.

Safety Jack Tatum, one of the most feared hitters in NFL history, broke on the play, reaching Fuqua at the same instant the ball did and causing a collision that sent the ball careening to the rookie Harris, who was 25 feet away.

"I was always taught to go to the ball, so when [Bradshaw] threw it, that's what I did," recounted Harris. "The next thing I knew, the ball was coming right to me. The rest has always been a blur."

That blur was Harris racing down the sideline and scoring the winning, and much disputed, touchdown. Disputed because the rules at the time said that if the ball ricocheted off the intended receiver, in this case Fuqua, then no other Steeler could touch it until after a defender did.

Tatum said the ball didn't touch him. Raiders executive Al LoCasale, who had an unobstructed view from the sideline, said it never touched Tatum. And at the time of the play it seemed like the officials didn't think it touched Tatum either. Instead of ruling it a touchdown, referee Fred Swearingen consulted with his crew of officials and then went into the dugout at Three Rivers Stadium to call Art McNally, the NFL's supervisor of officials.

Several minutes later, and after an announcement was circulating around the press box that the officials were consulting the videotape—fourteen years before instant replay became policy—Swearingen surfaced from the dugout and signaled touchdown.

John Madden, the coach of the Raiders from 1969 to 1978, never understood what happened. "If it was a touchdown, why didn't they call it a touchdown right away? And how did [Swearingen] know it was a touchdown after he went and talked on the phone? I've never gotten over it and I never will."

Neither did Al Davis, who still swears up and down that the ball went off Fuqua—the one and only man involved in the play not proffering an opinion.

Decades later John Fetkovich, an emeritus professor of physics at Carnegie Mellon University and longtime Steelers fan, analyzed the videotape and conducted a series of experiments on rebounding footballs. And using the fundamental laws of physics, conservation of momentum and coefficient of restitution, he concluded that the correct call was made.

Al Davis, however, continues to respectfully disagree with Sir Isaac Newton.

Double-Sided Coin

November 26, 1998: Steelers at Lions

The coin toss has been around since pro football began in 1892. Only then, it was done by the team captains. It wasn't until 1921 that the referees got involved. But after Thanksgiving Day 1998, there were probably more than a few players and fans in Pittsburgh who longed for a return to the nineteenth century.

The opening coin toss is the most mundane component of an NFL football game. The overtime coin toss, however, can be the difference between winning and losing.

With the score tied 16-16, the Lions' and Steelers' captains gathered at midfield for Phil Luckett's overtime coin toss. Jerome Bettis made the call, tails—according to him and television replays that would run every hour on the hour for the duration of the holiday weekend—but when the coin came up tails, Luckett awarded the ball to the hometown Lions, who quickly turned their good fortune into a 42-yard game-winning field goal.

Explaining the decision to Pittsburgh's perpetually prognathous head coach Bill Cowher, Luckett said, "[Bettis] said heads-tails. And I'm going with heads because that was his first call."

Bettis called Luckett's claim a "bold-faced lie." And Cowher complained, more diplomatically, that even if Bettis did change his call, he did it before the coin hit the ground. But if that was the case, then Cowher, Bettis, and the Steelers had no case.

The Official Playing Rules of the NFL reads: *A captain's first choice from any alternative privileges which may be offered his team, before or during the game, is final and not subject to change.*

So technically, Luckett was in the right. Although he did have another option, apart from holding firm to his decision and causing the controversial cloud that hangs over his head to this day. He could have re-tossed the coin.

Jerry Seeman, the director of NFL officiating who was responsible for reviewing the incident, admitted that once, when he was working a game in Houston, he tossed a coin that landed diagonally against a player's foot. Upon calling "heads," and then hearing about it from the team that had tails, Seeman decided to toss the coin again.

Luckett decided against that, and he's been living with that decision ever since, a decision that cost him a playoff game later that postseason. To avoid further controversy the NFL sent him a playoff game check of $9,800, but declined to give him a postseason assignment.

The league also immediately changed the specifics of its coin toss rules for the first time in twenty years. Players must now make a definitive call before the coin is tossed. And after escorting the team captains in from the sidelines, the field and back judges are required to stay at midfield for the toss's duration.

Call it "Luckett's Law"—to coin a phrase.

Footballs Are Brown
December 6, 1998: Seahawks at Jets

We don't have an axe to grind with Phil Luckett. Even though most of upstate New York would like to see "The Music City Miracle" make this list—it was Phil Luckett who passed down judgment from the replay monitor and declared Frank Wycheck's lateral to Kevin Dyson legal, knocking the Bills from the playoffs—we happen to believe that in January of 2000 he made the right call.

But in December of 1998, just twelve days after the Thanksgiving Day coin-flip flap, Luckett was in the middle of another mess. Although to be fair, if instant replay had been around during the '98 season, this bad call would have probably been corrected.

Vinny Testaverde spent that entire Sunday afternoon dropping back to pass, throwing the ball a then-career-high 63 times. But with 20 seconds on the clock, the Jets trailing by 5, and facing a fourth-and-goal from the Seattle 5-yard line, Testaverde made the play of the game with his feet, following center Kevin Mawae in for the game-winning quarterback draw.

At least that's what it looked like from head linesman Earnie Frantz's view. What everyone else saw, and what happened in reality, was Testaverde getting tackled short of the goal line and only the crown of his helmet breaking its plane. The football, clutched firmly and securely near Testaverde's waist, was a full two feet shy of the end zone.

Phil Luckett immediately ran into the pile to try to sort through the throng of bodies. But Frantz, mimicking the ten other Jets on the field and the 70,000 Jets fans in the stands, signaled touchdown.

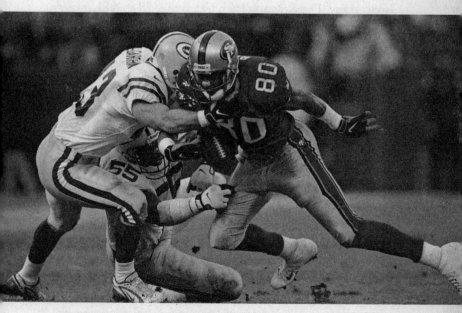

1999 Playoffs, Packers at 49ers: Jerry Rice is ruled down even though the football is clearly fumbled before his knee hits the ground.

Perhaps Luckett was gun shy after all of the second guessing he'd just endured on Thanksgiving Day. Or maybe it was a simple case of loyalty to his head linesman. Whatever his reason, the result was the same. Despite the power and obligation to make things right, Luckett chose to let Frantz's incorrect and game-deciding call stand.

A day later the Seahawks got an apology from the league and an official explanation from NFL director of officiating, Jerry Seeman. Earnie Frantz saw Testaverde's (white) helmet break the plane of the goal line and thought it was the (brown) football.

As a result of Frantz's color confusion, the unlucky losing Seahawks missed the playoffs by one game. And as a result of that, head coach Dennis Erickson lost his job.

There was, however, some good to come out of Seattle's ill-fated misery. Three months later, by a vote of 28-3, NFL owners brought back instant replay.

Rice Krispied Pack
January 3, 1999: NFC Wildcard, Packers at 49ers

Terrell Owens's catch at the goal line between two Packers defenders to win a playoff game in the closing seconds is one of the greatest postseason moments of all time. And if you don't believe us, just ask T. O. But it also happens to be a great play that never should have been.

In response to a series of questionable calls during the 1998 regular season, most notably the two that you just read about involving Phil Luckett, the NFL discussed the idea of instituting an instant replay system for the playoffs. But the league's competition committee, of which then-Packers coach Mike Holmgren was cochair, rejected the idea. Which, as you will soon see, is the height of irony.

Trailing Green Bay 27-23, the ball at the Packers 47-yard line, and with just 40 seconds to play, the future Hall of Fame connection of Steve Young and Jerry Rice hooked up on a 6-yard completion—Rice's first catch of the game. But before Rice could pick up significant yardage or get out of bounds to stop the clock, he was stripped of the ball by safety Scott McGarrahan. Green Bay linebacker Bernardo Harris then pounced on the loose football, and the Packers had their fourth straight playoff win over San Francisco.

But playing the role of party pooper that Sunday—with a complicit assist from field judge Kevin Mack—was line judge Jeff Bergman, who cut the Packers' celebration short by instead ruling that Rice's knee was down before the ball came out. There was no fumble.

After all, this was San Francisco. Rice is the greatest wide receiver of all time. And to turn him into a playoff goat on his one and only catch of the afternoon would be unforgivable.

We're not saying that any of that was a factor in Bergman's ruling, and in Mack's decision to let the call stand despite a better, and unobstructed, view of the play. But had Bergman called it a fumble, or even worse in the eyes of Niners fans, had Mack overruled him, imagine the effigies the pair would have passed on their way to the airport.

So the completion to Rice stood. And four plays later the devastated and suddenly disorganized Packers defense, with extreme prejudice attached, gave Owens his moment of glory and the Niners the comeback win.

Packers G.M. Ron Wolf didn't mince words in the postgame press conference, telling reporters, "It was clearly a fumble, we clearly recovered, game over."

But Niners quarterback Steve Young, who had sustained several serious concussions by this point in his career, making him an appreciably less than reliable witness, said, "It was clearly NOT a fumble."

The television replay of the call in question bears Wolf's claims out. But his continuing comments that included the phrase, "We're for instant replay and we always will be," were somewhat laughable. It was, after all, Wolf's own coach who stood in the way of implementing the system that would have had his team advancing in the playoffs instead of going home.

Maybe in time Wolf will grow to appreciate the irony. Or maybe not.

"The Big Lie"
January 1, 1978: AFC Championship, Raiders at Broncos

Raiders owner Al Davis has been convinced for years that there is an NFL commissioner's office conspiracy to keep his team out of the Super Bowl. We've addressed the "Tuck Rule." Many Raiders fans also take issue with the non-call on Tony Siragusa when he took out Rich Gannon in the 2001 AFC Championship Game. And for years there have been complaints about the disproportionate number of cold-weather games the Raiders get scheduled. But the origin of Al's conspiracy theory is January 1, 1978, at Mile High Stadium.

Prior to 1977 the Denver Broncos had recorded just three winning seasons in seventeen years of existence. And the most consistent loser of the AFL's original eight franchises had never won a division title or played in a postseason game. So everyone, especially the city of Denver, was stunned to see the Broncos on top of the division with a 12-2 record and entering the AFC Championship Game on New Year's Day 1978, just one step away from the Super Bowl.

On the backs of the "Orange Crush" defense that sent five of its members to the Pro Bowl later that month, Denver held a 7-3 lead in the third quarter and was threatening to score again. But before the Broncos could extend that lead to 14-3, fullback Rob

Lytle coughed up the ball at the goal line after a hit from Raiders safety Jack Tatum. Defensive lineman Mike McCoy picked up the loose pigskin and began to head the other way for a possible 14-point swing in Oakland's favor—when the play was blown dead.

The ruling: Lytle was down—even though every replay showed that the ball popped out long before Lytle made his leap toward the goal line. So instead of a touchdown for the Raiders, the officials gave the Broncos a second chance at the end zone. A second chance that Denver took full advantage of when Jon Keyworth scored one play later.

In the locker room after the game, the Raiders players expressed outrage about the call. And when John Madden was pressed by reporters to give his opinion, he reacted angrily, "Hell yes, it was a fumble. Twenty million people saw it."

Owner Al Davis took it one step further, claiming that while the officials were conferring on the play, Commissioner Pete Rozelle actually sent someone from his office down to the field to tell the referee how to rule, calling the decision and its official explanation (Lytle's forward progress had been stopped) "The Big Lie."

The Rozelle-Davis feud born that day would haunt the league for years to come. In 1980 the Raiders owner sued the NFL for blocking his planned move south to Los Angeles. Davis won the case, settling for $18 million in damages and winning the right to move his team to the L.A. Coliseum in time for the 1982 season.

And in 1986, taking another swing at Rozelle, Davis testified against the commissioner and his fellow owners—and on behalf of the USFL—in that league's $1.7 billion antitrust lawsuit against the NFL. In exchange for Davis's testimony, the USFL agreed to not name him or the Raiders as a codefendant.

On July 24, 1986, the courts awarded the USFL a whole $3 in damages, effectively ending its existence.

Wide Right?

December 26, 1965: NFL Western Conference Playoffs,
Colts at Packers

The Colts-Packers 1965 playoff game featured just about everything. The hallowed grounds of the newly named Lambeau Field. A pair of future Hall of Fame coaches in Vince Lombardi and Don Shula, who at the time was only thirty-five and in just his third season. Two future Hall of Famers at quarterback, although both Johnny Unitas and Bart Starr were reduced to spectator roles because of injury. And a controversial ending that to this day keeps most of the old-time Colts fans up at night.

In 1965 the NFL didn't have the series of formulas that it now uses to break ties and award playoff spots. In the days before league eggheads created the algorithms "strength of schedule" and "best net points in common games," standings' stalemates were settled on the field. And after identical 10-3-1 seasons, the Packers and Colts gathered on this post-Christmas Day Sunday to break their Western Division log jam and send one of them on to face the Browns in the NFL Championship. The Super Bowl wouldn't begin until the following season.

The short-handed Colts—Johnny Unitas was out with a knee injury and his backup, Gary Cuozzo, was sidelined with a dislocated shoulder—were forced to start running back Tom Matte at quarterback, the position he played at Ohio State. The Packers, minus Bart Starr after he went down on the first play of the game with injured ribs, had backup Zeke Bratkowski under center.

Bratkowski, an actual quarterback, completed 22 passes for 248 yards on the day. Matte, on the other hand, completed just five. But somehow it was Matte's Colts that were leading 10-7 with less than two minutes to play when Don Chandler was setting up to kick a game-tying 22-yard field goal.

Immediately after striking the ball, Chandler snapped his

head back in disgust and kicked the dirt. Baltimore defensive tackle Ordell Brasse began to clap his hands in celebration of the missed kick. But both men were only reacting to the ball, which by all accounts was sailing wide right above the short goal posts. By all accounts except the one given by field judge Jim Tunney, who called the kick good.

"There were a lot of sighs from the crowd like it didn't go through," Matte remembered. "And then there were cheers when they looked at the official."

While the angry Colts argued their case to the referees, to no avail of course, Chandler got an earful from an irate Lombardi, who in no uncertain language told his kicker to never, ever react negatively to a kick again. Even, and especially, when the kick was no good.

Thanks to Tunney's gift, the Packers went on to win the game 13-10 on a without-a-doubt 25-yard Chandler field goal 13:39 into overtime. And a week later Green Bay beat Cleveland for its first of three straight NFL Championships.

The Colts, not quick to forgive or forget, took out their frustrations the following week in the NFL's short-lived and ridiculously conceived "Third Place Game" by dismantling the Cowboys 35-3.

The very next season, and in response to the controversy, the NFL standardized its goalposts, painting them bright yellow and lengthening the uprights.

And just in case there are some of you who think that time does in fact heal all wounds: When Don Shula was asked about Chandler's kick in 1993, as he was on the verge of becoming the NFL's all-time winningest head coach, he replied unflinchingly, "It was a bad call. He clearly missed it. It was a game that propelled Lombardi to his great accomplishments; and it's a game we should have won."

And that anger still existed after twenty-eight years, 307 wins, and six Super Bowls.

Colts' Counterfeit Comeback
October 6, 2003: Colts at Buccaneers

Is there anything in sports as celebrated or enduring as a great comeback victory? Especially when the comeback happens on that sport's national stage, and is orchestrated by its newest favorite son.

Peyton Manning went into the 2003 season with a reputation off the field as spotless as his freshly laundered road-white Colts uniform. But on the field the NFL's golden boy was wearing the uncomfortable label of "Can't Win the Big One." Manning had lost his previous two games on Monday night and was 0-3 all-time in postseason play, coming off a 41-0 Wildcard beat down against the Jets.

But during a four-minute stretch in Tampa on Monday, October 6, 2003, Manning officially chucked that monkey off his back when he led Indianapolis to one of the greatest comebacks in NFL history.

Trailing 35-14, Indianapolis's late fourth-quarter surge began with a fourth-down 3-yard touchdown run by James Mungro. A successful onside kick followed with 3:37 to play, which eventually led to a Manning-to-Marvin Harrison 28-yard TD strike—and a 35-28 score with 2:27 on the clock.

The next onside try by the Colts' special teams proved fruitless. But Indy's 10th-ranked defense followed up that failure with a huge 3-and-out stop, putting the ball back in the hands of its 3rd-ranked offense with 1:41 left. Five plays later, and two plays after Manning hooked up on a 52-yard pass to Harrison, Ricky Williams plunged in for a closing-seconds game-tying touchdown.

Capping the comeback, and securing the Colts as the talk of the town, was a 29-yard overtime field goal by Mike Vanderjagt.

It was the kind of win that legends are made from. Songs are written and sung by little kids. Lunchbox depictions are cast in steel. And before you know it, two million football fans are claiming that they occupied one of the 66,000 seats at Raymond James Stadium that night.

But in reality the entire comeback was a fraud perpetrated by incompetent referees.

First, the onside kick with 3:37 to play. According to NFL Rule 10, Section 1, Article 4, in order for the kicking team (Indianapolis) to legally recover the football after it travels 10 yards, it must either hit the ground or touch a member of the receiving team (Tampa Bay).

Vanderjagt's kick did neither, making it an *illegal* play. Instead of another possession for Manning—and another touchdown in Indy's remarkable rally—the illegitimate kick should have resulted in a 15-yard penalty and a Bucs possession deep in Indianapolis territory. Which would have then presumably salted away the win for Tampa Bay.

The following week, NFL Director of Officiating Mike Pereira made the outrageous admission that his crew working the game didn't misinterpret the onside-kick rule. They didn't even know it.

But that's not all.

Just in case the Colts couldn't close the deal following that egregious gift of stupidity, the refs did Indy another favor in overtime. Before Vanderjagt's game-winning field goal sent the Bucs home as luckless losers, he actually missed it. But an unsportsmanlike "leaping" penalty was called on Simeon Rice that gave Vanderjagt another and ultimately successful attempt.

Pereira didn't admit any wrongdoing by his crew on the application of NFL Rule 12, Section 3, Article 2, which makes it illegal for one player to "leap" in an attempt to block a field goal and then land on another player. But Monday Night Football's Al Michaels made his thoughts on the penalty quite clear.

Upon hearing the referee call "leaping," Michaels exclaimed, "What is that? That's an unbelievable call!"

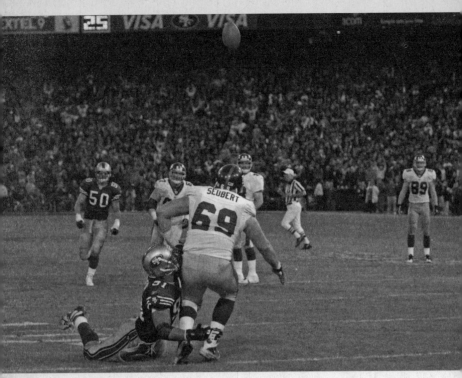

2003 Playoffs, Giants at 49ers: The Giants' Rich Seubert is tackled (interfered with) by the 49ers' Chike Okeafor on the game's final play.

Giant Wildcard Wipeout

January 5, 2003: NFC Wildcard, Giants at 49ers

Sure, the Giants blew a 24-point lead on their way to losing the Wildcard game against the 49ers, 39-38, but it's a whole lot more fun to blame the officials. Especially when the league comes out the very next day and admits they screwed up.

In 2002 the NFL added the Houston Texans as its thirty-second franchise, forcing the league to realign into eight divisions of four teams. Aside from the split into North and South divisions and the Colts getting bumped from the AFC East, where they had been since the division was created in 1970, the biggest changes came in the NFC West.

The Falcons, Saints, and Panthers all migrated to the South and were replaced by the Cardinals, a longtime East resident, and the Seahawks, who for twenty-four years took up roost in the AFC after their inaugural 1976 season placement in the NFC West.

Only the Rams and 49ers remained from a season ago. But tradition still ruled the day when San Francisco won its fourteenth division title in twenty-one years with a 10-6 record, setting up a first-round playoff game at home against the Giants.

New York appeared to be rolling toward an easy victory, up 38-14 late in the third quarter, when the wheels suddenly and dramatically came off. Over the final 17 minutes of play, the 49ers put together scoring drives of 70, 74, and 68 yards; they averaged just 1:42 in completing three touchdown drives; and twice Jeff Garcia and Terrell Owens hooked up for 2-point conversions. Topping off the New York frustration was safety Shaun Williams's punch and ejection following the Niners' lead-taking touchdown.

But despite all of that—their near total and complete collapse—the Giants found themselves lined up for a potential winning 41-yard field goal on the game's final play.

With regular season long-snapper Dan O'Leary out injured, the Giants had asked 41-year-old Trey Junkin just five days earlier to end his month-long retirement and take over the duties in O'Leary's absence. A decision by Junkin that he later said he'd give anything to have back.

Junkin's snap was low and away, and it couldn't be handled cleanly by holder Matt Allen. In the free-for-all that followed, and in a desperate move to salvage the busted play, Allen threw the ball downfield to guard Rich Seubert. But before the 305-pound Seubert could catch the ball, he was tackled by the Niners' equally hefty Chike Okeafor for obvious pass interference.

Three flags were thrown on the play, and 49ers coach Steve Mariucci confessed later that he was expecting to have interference be the call. But instead, all three flags were thrown on Giants guard Tam Hopkins for being illegally down field—which was, incidentally, a correct call. When referee Ron Winter was asked after the game why he didn't also call pass interference on Okeafor, Winter explained, "Because the receiver was ineligible."

Unfortunately for the Giants, Ron Winter got his guards crossed. Seubert, the guard that was interfered with by Okeafor, had in fact reported as eligible. Meaning that the play should have resulted in offsetting penalties and a second field goal attempt for the Giants. Instead, because of Winter's confusion the Giants get a place on the short end of the second biggest playoff comeback in NFL history.

League apologist and NFL Director of Officiating Mike Pereira did acknowledge Winter's mistake the following day. But with San Francisco moving on and New York heading home, Giants head coach Jim Fassel, in an unforgiving mood, responded, "[Pereira's apology] doesn't do us a damn bit of good."

Theft at Three Rivers
January 6, 1980: AFC Championship, Oilers at Steelers

The NFL didn't begin using instant replay to correct officiating mistakes until 1986. But the moment the league actually began to seriously discuss the idea took place six years earlier, during the AFC Championship Game in Pittsburgh.

A lot of people don't remember just how good the Houston Oilers of the late 1970s were because most of us remember them as one of the most fun and entertaining teams of that decade. It was the era of Luv Ya Blue, the stick-in-your-brain fight song "Houston Oilers Number One," and Bum Phillips's ten-gallon hat—a colorful head coach who once quipped that the reason his team didn't scrimmage during training camp was because "Houston's not on our schedule."

But this team could also play football.

Following a wildcard run to the AFC Championship Game

after the 1978 season, the Oilers were ready for an encore in 1979. And Houston fans got it to the tune of an 11-5 record, a first-ever Thanksgiving Day win over in-state rival Dallas, and a memorable victory over Oakland that featured the lasting image of Earl Campbell, rocked back on his heels at the 1-yard line on a hit from safety Jack Tatum, turning, stumbling backwards, and still scoring the go-ahead touchdown. A highlight that to this day defines the power that took the Heisman Trophy-winning Campbell to five Pro Bowls and the Pro Football Hall of Fame.

The Oilers' 1979 season of successes erased the bitter memories of that January's embarrassing 34-5 Championship Game loss to Pittsburgh and set Houston up for a rematch of redemption twelve months later back at Three Rivers Stadium.

And this time, there would be no blowout. In fact, trailing the defending champs 17-10 in the third quarter, the underdog Oilers drove the ball all the way to the Pittsburgh 6-yard line with a chance to tie things up with a touchdown. And when quarterback Dan Pastorini lobbed a perfect pass to second-year wide receiver Mike Renfro in the back of the end zone, it looked like Houston had done just that. But looks can be deceiving.

The two officials who had position at the back of the end zone stared at each other, frozen for a few seconds, clearly hoping that the other one would put his neck on the line and make the call. And finally, unsure if Renfro had secured the ball with both feet inbounds, side judge Donald Orr made the uncertain, and as it turned out, erroneous ruling of incomplete.

Television replays showed that Renfro indeed had clear possession and both feet down. But this was 1980, when replays only served to inflame the ire of the slighted football fan, while simultaneously vilifying the offending official. Nothing could be done about the mistake, and the Oilers had to settle for a field goal. A 4-point difference that stole Houston's momentum and eventually carried Pittsburgh to a 27-13 win—and two weeks later its fourth Super Bowl title in six years.

1975 Playoffs, Cowboys at Vikings: After pushing Vikings defensive back Nate Wright to the ground, Drew Pearson scores the Cowboys' game-winning touchdown.

The NFL, humbled and embarrassed by the controversy in such an important game, and anxious to find a remedy, began to recognize the potential of television instant replay.

The Oilers, never as angry as they had the right to be, returned home to an Astrodome rally with 70,000 screaming fans, where Bum Phillips delivered this impassioned promise: "One year ago, we knocked on the door. This year, we beat on the door. Next year, we're gonna kick the son of a bitch in."

They never did.

Pearson's Push, and the First Hail Mary
December 28, 1975: NFC Divisional Playoff, Cowboys at Vikings

The year 1975 was one for innovations. *Saturday Night Live* changed the face of late-night television; Arthur Ashe made history at Wimbledon, ushering in a new era in tennis; and the NFL saw the creation of its most popular game-ending play, the Hail Mary pass. It's ironic, however, that the first "official" Hail Mary should have actually been an offensive penalty.

After losing the previous two Super Bowls, and three in five years, the Vikings believed that 1975 was finally going to be their year. They began the season with ten straight wins, finished with a 12-2 record, and went into the playoffs with the league's number-one-ranked defense, one of the best of all time, "The Purple People Eaters."

The Cowboys had their own pretty good "Doomsday Defense," and Roger Staubach to counter Fran Tarkenton. But with twelve rookies on its 43-man roster, and the game being played on Metropolitan Stadium's frozen turf, Dallas entered the Divisional playoff as 7-point underdogs.

The game unfolded, as expected, as a defensive struggle. The Vikings took a 7-0 lead on a 1-yard Chuck Foreman touchdown in the second quarter. The Cowboys tied it in the third quarter on a 4-yard run by Doug Dennison, and then took the lead in the fourth when Toni Fritsch, an Austrian soccer star brought to the NFL by Tom Landry, kicked a 24-yard field goal.

After a late touchdown by Brent McClanahan reclaimed the lead for Minnesota, 14-10, Staubach and the Cowboys got the ball back on their own 15 with just 1:51 on the clock. Which is precisely when the game took a turn to the completely unexpected.

Most people can picture the 50-yard bomb Staubach threw to Drew Pearson to win the game. But before that, when Dallas was facing a 4th-and-16 from its own 25, Staubach and

Pearson hooked up for a 25-yard game-saving completion that put the ball at midfield. A play that was every bit as important in the Cowboys' comeback, though not as historical as what it set up.

With 24 ticks left on the clock, and the Cowboys out of timeouts, Staubach unleashed the Hail Mary (as described by him to reporters postgame) deep down the right side of the field. Pearson, being shadowed by cornerback Nate Wright, immediately recognized that against the stiff stadium winds the ball was going to come up short.

Adjusting to its flight, and achieving separation from Wright with what Pearson described later as a "swim move"—which had the ancillary effect of knocking Wright to the ground—Pearson was able to pin the ball between his elbow and hip and run the final 5 yards for the winning touchdown.

Angered, incensed, and in disbelief that offensive pass interference wasn't called, Vikings safety Paul Krause immediately began to scream at field judge Armen Terzian for the non-call. Head coach Bud Grant and the rest of the Vikings were soon to follow, and before you knew it, garbage, including a variety of whiskey bottles, began raining down on the field.

One of the errant airborne bottles, known in the Twin Cities as the game's *true* Hail Mary, nailed Terzian in the head and knocked him unconscious for several minutes. Terzian was able to leave the field with only superficial wounds, but sadly the same couldn't be said for Tarkenton.

Shortly after the gut-wrenching loss, the future Hall of Famer found out that his father, who incidentally was named Dallas, had suffered a fatal heart attack while watching the game from his Georgia home.

Contrary to popular myth, Dallas Tarkenton Sr. was stricken during the third quarter, before the controversial play.

Bert and the Bucs Lose by a Nose

January 23, 2000: NFC Championship, Buccaneers at Rams

We don't begrudge officials when the bad calls they make are actually just by-products of bad league rules. Like Supreme Court Justices, the referee's job is to interpret law, not make it. But simply recognizing that the true guilty party may reside somewhere above the man wearing stripes and carrying a whistle doesn't exempt them from our list.

The year 1999 was a crazy one in the NFL. Y2K panic was in full swing. And fearing that the millennium bug that would soon turn our credit cards into plastic Braille drink coasters would also take down pro football, the NFL moved its schedule back a week.

As originally planned, the first playoff games were to be played on Saturday, January 1, 2000. But that date became off limits. So even when that first weekend in January became the regular season's Week 17, the NFL broke form and left Saturday off its schedule.

Thankfully, other than the 14,000 times we were all subjected to Prince's "1999," Armageddon didn't occur. But the NFL did have its own version of the end of the world when little-known Arena Football League quarterback Kurt Warner won the MVP award with forty-one touchdown passes and four teams that had never won a Super Bowl advanced to the conference championship games.

As great as the season was, the NFC Championship Game, featuring the Bucs and Rams, was far from a thing of beauty. Warner's Greatest Show on Turf managed to score just one touchdown, and not until the fourth quarter. The two quarterbacks combined to throw five interceptions. The teams combined for five fumbles. And the special teams combined to kick nine punts. It was a terrible 59 minutes of football.

But in the last minute . . .

Trailing the Rams 11-6, quarterback Shaun King finally found his rhythm, driving his offense into St. Louis territory with under a minute to play. After taking a sack back at the 35, King hit wide receiver Bert Emanuel at the 22, and then immediately called timeout to set up Tampa's 3rd-and-10 play.

But during that timeout, and with replay back in vogue, the officials determined that even though Emanuel clearly had possession with both hands, the nose of the ball touched the turf as he was diving for the catch, and that made it an incomplete pass. A decision that cost the Bucs 13 yards, a critical down, and a timeout. Instead of facing 3rd-and-10 from the 22, the ball was moved back to the 35-yard line for an unrecoverable 3rd-and-23.

In announcing his ruling to the crowd, Referee Bill Carollo said, "It was apparent that the player, as he was catching the ball, used the ground. The tip of the ball hit the ground. And because the ball hit the ground, by rule it's an automatic incomplete pass."

Automatic being the key word.

It didn't matter that Emanuel had clear possession. If any part of the ball touched the ground—which it did—then the pass had to be ruled incomplete—which it was. Carollo was simply following the letter of the law.

A law that was changed the very next year in response to the Bucs getting robbed of their chance to make it to the Super Bowl.

Now, all a receiver has to do is demonstrate possession of the ball. The ground no longer matters. And when a team takes a timeout after what is eventually ruled an incomplete pass by replay, they get the timeout back.

Both commonsense moves by the NFL that came a season too late for Tampa Bay.

Free Jackie Smith
January 21, 1979: Super Bowl XIII, Cowboys vs. Steelers

The official position of whipping boy—a child that was raised in England's royal court alongside the crown prince for the express purpose of being punished and beaten when the prince did wrong—was retired during the eighteenth century. But unofficially the practice was revived in Dallas, Texas, in 1979.

The current, and most notorious, whipping boy not named Bill Buckner is Jackie Smith. The Pro Football Hall of Famer, who retired as the NFL's all-time receiver among tight ends with 480 receptions, has unfairly borne that burden because of the one pass he didn't catch—a touchdown in Super Bowl XIII.

What makes it unfair is that his infamous end-zone drop happened in the third quarter, and the Cowboys still had ample opportunity to win it in the fourth. And they may have done just that, and Smith might only be known as one of the all-time greats of the game, if not for an extremely questionable pass-interference call.

Many people considered Super Bowl XIII to be the best of all time. It matched the defending champion Cowboys, America's Team, against the Steelers, the team of the decade. This game featured nineteen players on the way to the Pro Bowl later that month, fourteen players who would eventually make their way to the Hall of Fame, and a pair of future Hall of Fame coaches in Tom Landry and Chuck Noll.

After several big plays, including three touchdown passes (28, 75, and 7 yards) by Terry Bradshaw, a pair of long touchdowns by the Cowboys, and Smith's noted dropped pass, the Steelers held on to a 21-17 fourth-quarter lead. With both offenses moving the ball, the game was anyone's.

On a 2nd-and-5 play from his own 44, Bradshaw went for the jugular with a deep ball to Lynn Swann down the right side of the field. As Swann and cornerback Benny Barnes ran together stride for stride, Barnes tripped over his own feet and fell. And unable to avoid the Cowboy that was now lying in his path, Swann went down as well.

It seemed like the perfect time for a no-call. It was a simple case of two guys getting their legs tangled as they both looked back for the football. But that's not how field judge Fred Swearingen saw it. He instantly threw the flag and called a punishing 33-yard pass interference penalty on Barnes.

Barnes, fuming about the call because he thought Swann pushed him, cussed at Swearingen—and then concluded that since he didn't get in trouble for that, Swearingen must have known that he got the call wrong.

Swearingen would only tell reporters afterward, "It was a judgment call."

Of course, by then none of it mattered. Two plays after the penalty, Franco Harris scored to put Pittsburgh up an insurmountable 28-17. Three more touchdowns were scored in the fourth quarter, and the Cowboys were able to make the final score a respectable 35-31, but the winning margin could be traced directly back to Swearingen's untimely flag.

The specifics of "incidental contact" were added to the NFL rulebook the following year, and *Sports Illustrated* did a lengthy article on the game-turning pass-interference penalty. But somehow, still, it was Jackie Smith who emerged from Miami as the "Super Bowl Goat."

Two-Eyed Monster
January 14, 1996: AFC Championship, Colts at Steelers

It was French Emperor Napoleon Bonaparte who said, "History is a set of lies agreed upon."

Normally we wouldn't quote a deranged and diminutive

dictator, but Napoleon's words demonstrate the historical fable that has become the 1995 AFC Championship Game.

History teaches us that the Colts lost to the Steelers that day because Jim Harbaugh's last-gasp Hail Mary slipped out of Aaron Bailey's hands as he hit the end-zone turf. But in fact, Indianapolis met its Waterloo on a blown call back in the second quarter. A game-deciding play that for too long has gone unmentioned by worst-call watchdogs.

The 1995 Colts, in reality, had no business even making it to the AFC Championship Game. They didn't qualify for the playoffs until a Week 17 victory against New England. They wouldn't have gotten past the Chargers in the Wildcard game if it hadn't been for four Stan Humphries interceptions. And if it weren't for three Steve Bono interceptions and a pair of chip-shot missed field goals by Lin Elliott, they wouldn't have handed the top-seeded Chiefs their only loss of the year in Kansas City.

But all of those things did happen. And quarterback Jim Harbaugh, the man who was humiliated by Mike Ditka, cut by the Bears, and benched by the Colts, pulled off one of the great magic acts in all of sports: getting the league's 23rd-ranked offense to Pittsburgh within one win of the Super Bowl.

Most of the Championship Game's first half was a battle of field goals, favoring Indianapolis 6-3. But late in the second quarter, only 13 seconds before halftime, missed-call misfortune struck. With Neil O'Donnell scrambling to find an open receiver on a 3rd-and-goal play, rookie Kordell Stewart (in his "Slash" days as a QB/WR/RB) broke free from double-coverage in the back of the end zone, where O'Donnell hit him for the touchdown.

One big problem. As Stewart was running around Colts safety Jason Belser along the end line to get open, he ran out of bounds. And that act, unseen by field judge John Robinson, the official closest to the play, made Stewart an ineligible receiver.

Instead of a Pittsburgh touchdown, it should have been a penalty that forced a Pittsburgh field goal. A 4-point difference that just happened to make up the margin of victory in the Steelers' eventual 20-16 win.

Take away those four points, and instead of Jim Harbaugh's final-play 29-yard Hail Mary toss to Aaron Bailey, the Colts would have trotted out kicker Cary Blanchard for a possible game-winning field goal attempt.

And even if Blanchard missed, the worst the Colts would have been facing was overtime.

After the game, when faced with the replays of Stewart's touchdown, referee Bernie Kukar admitted to the mistake, but said Robinson could have only seen the foul if he'd been looking down at Stewart's feet. Kukar then further tried to defend his erring official, but instead crossed headfirst into the land of ridiculous statements by adding, "Unfortunately he only has two eyes."

Unfortunate for everyone but, perhaps, Mrs. Robinson.

No Average Joe
January 8, 1984: NFC Championship, 49ers at Redskins

Sometimes bad calls are the result of poorly written rules. Other times, the officials tasked with enforcement simply misinterpret them. And on occasion, the referee in charge mistakenly interprets the wrong rule.

But in this instance, on a play that quite possibly kept Joe Montana out of a fifth Super Bowl, the referees forgot to apply a newly written rule.

Anyone who puts together a list of the NFL's best teams of all time has to give serious consideration to ranking the 1983 Washington Redskins number one. They scored a then-record 541 points, posted an incredible turnover ratio of plus-43, lost a total of two regular season games by one point each, and six times they won games by a margin of at least three touchdowns.

And let's not forget their 51-7 pasting of the Rams in the opening round of the playoffs.

So it wasn't really that surprising, outside of San Francisco, when Washington dominated the first three quarters of their NFC Championship meeting with the 49ers, and went into the fourth quarter up a commanding 21-0.

Although, considering his status as the MVP of Super Bowl XVI, the comeback that the then-27-year-old Joe Montana orchestrated should have also surprised no one.

Early in the fourth quarter Montana got things started for the Niners with a 23-yard touchdown pass to wide receiver Mike Wilson. Then after the Redskins missed a field goal, Montana hit Freddie Solomon for a 76-yard touchdown that made the score 21-14. And finally, with 7:08 remaining, the comeback was complete. Montana hit Wilson again, this time from 12 yards out, to knot things up at 21-all.

The Redskins were reeling, and the Niners were rolling. And everyone in the stadium knew that if Montana got the ball back in his hands, the record-setting season in Washington would end right there.

The Redskins took over at their own 22, hoping to play a game of keep-away while trying to move themselves downfield for the winning score. And initially, Skins quarterback Joe Theismann was doing just that, driving his offense to the San Francisco 45. But on a 2nd-and-10 pass, deep down the sideline, the drive was close to stalling when Theismann's throw landed innocently incomplete.

But instead of the Niners defense being just one play away from giving the ball back to the red-hot Montana, Theismann and the Redskins' offense were bailed out by a terrible pass interference call.

Cornerback Eric Wright definitely made contact with wide receiver Art Monk. That's never been in dispute. But Theismann's pass landed a good five yards out of bounds, making it "uncatchable" and according to the official pass interference rules, newly rewritten in 1983, not a penalty.

But the penalty was called. And just in case overcoming that gift wasn't challenging enough for San Francisco, a few plays later on 3rd-and-10 safety Ronnie Lott was called for defensive holding, even though all he did was bump a jogging Charlie Brown 20 yards away from the play.

Already deep in San Francisco territory because of the interference call, the defensive holding penalty allowed Washington to run the clock down from more than two minutes to play to only 40 seconds before Mark Moseley came on to kick his 25-yard game-winning field goal.

Who knows what would have happened if the referees had not incorrectly called pass interference? Or if Montana's last-ditch drive that ultimately fell short had begun with the timeouts and 2 minutes that he should have had?

But we do know this. Not one person there that day would have bet against him.

Snowplowed

December 12, 1982: Dolphins at Patriots

Legendary comedian Carl Reiner said that he finds snow "to be an unnecessary freezing of water." Football fans in south Florida would probably take their distaste for the white, translucent frozen precipitation one or two steps further.

Because of the fifty-seven-day players' strike in 1982 and the major changes that it forced in the league's schedule—most notably a reduction from sixteen games down to nine—the NFL altered its postseason format. Division standings were suspended for the year, with the expanded field of sixteen playoff teams coming solely from their one-through-eight seedings within the conference.

December 12, 1982, Dolphins at Patriots: Mark Henderson, on work-release from prison, plowed the Patriots to victory in the snow.

That meant that not only did every win count double, so did every error.

In the December game between the Dolphins and Patriots, and on a field that featured some of the worst winter whiteout conditions ever seen in Foxboro, the two teams played almost sixty minutes of painful, brutal, scoreless football. Each team had attempted a field goal, and failed; and neither offense had come even remotely close to scoring a touchdown. But where there's a will, or a willing accomplice spending his weekends in a stadium on a work-release program from prison, there's a way.

With 4:45 remaining in regulation, the Patriots lined up for a 33-yard field goal. But with snow and ice covering the field, and the footing for a kicker next to impossible, Pats coach Ron Meyer called timeout so kicker John Smith could clear his spot.

"I saw John Smith on his hands and knees trying to get the snow cleared, and all of a sudden it hit me," recalled Meyer. "Why not send the snowplow out there?"

The snowplow (in actuality a snow sweeper) in question, driven by convicted felon Mark Henderson (fittingly of robbery), had been clearing the yard lines during timeouts all game. And as a man who knows how to take orders, Henderson had no problem with Meyer's request for him to clear a patch of ground around the 23-yard line.

Throwing the officials and the Dolphins off his plan, as any good criminal would do, Henderson went on the field and began to clear the 20-yard line without raising suspicions. But then, just as he reached the spot behind the ball, Henderson took a sudden turn left and cleared a perfect path of green for Smith to kick from.

The angry Dolphins saw what was happening, but as defensive tackle Bob Baumhower explained, there was nothing he could do. "I saw him coming. But no way am I going to take on a plow."

The referees, the people who should have had the power and wherewithal to stop Henderson, were just as impotent. During this theater of the absurd they stood idly by through Henderson's criminal clearing, Don Shula's caustic complaining, and Smith's critical game-winning kick.

In the end, the loss didn't cost the Dolphins. They went on to represent the AFC in the Super Bowl. But there was nothing benign about Henderson's ride into infamy—even though the Patriots treated it as such in 2001 when they invited the released and rehabilitated convict back for an encore reenactment during their final game at Foxboro Stadium.

By the margin of its stolen victory, New England made the playoffs in 1982, and Buffalo did not.

The Madness of Pete Morelli

January 15, 2006: AFC Divisional Playoffs, Steelers at Colts

Steelers linebacker Joey Porter called it conspiracy, telling reporters after Pittsburgh's Divisional Playoff game with the Colts, "I know [the officials] wanted Indy to win this game; the whole world loves Peyton Manning."

Conspiracy might be the wrong word. But lunacy, illogicality, and feebleminded folly are right on the money in describing the replay reversal that nearly stopped short Pittsburgh's run to Super Bowl XL.

All season long the Peyton Manning-led Colts were the darlings of the NFL. Not only was Manning the quarterback who had just one year earlier set the single-season touchdown-pass record at 49, the Colts were the team that started the 2005 season 13-0—putting a scare into the 1972 Dolphins, the NFL's only undefeated champion.

But everyone also loves an underdog. And that's what Pittsburgh was when it met Indianapolis for their first playoff matchup in nine years; and that's why so many fans were pleasantly stunned to see the Steelers dominating the top-seeded Colts 21-10 late in the fourth quarter.

With 5:26 left in regulation, and Peyton Manning needing to be perfect to get his team back in the game, his pass across the middle was picked off by the diving Troy Polamalu. As the Pittsburgh strong safety secured the ball firmly in both hands, and then got up to run, he dropped the ball, only to recover it himself immediately.

It was clearly a catch, fumble, and self-recovery; and thus it was clearly going to be Pittsburgh's ball at their own 48, and game over for Indianapolis. And because of the dire straits that that would put the Colts in, head coach Tony Dungy decided to throw his own Hail Mary pass by tossing out the challenge flag.

There was no way the play would get overturned—it was definitely a catch. But what did Dungy have to lose?

It was the perspicacious Mark Twain who said, "Get your facts first, and then you can distort them as much as you please." A direction followed to the letter by delusory referee Pete Morelli, who, when he emerged from under the replay hood where he had gathered the "facts," announced his distorted definition of an incomplete pass.

Answering Dungy's prayer, while simultaneously becoming the devil incarnate throughout Western Pennsylvania, Morelli overturned the interception, explaining, "[Polamalu] never had possession with his leg up off the ground, doing an act common to the game of football."

Never mind Morelli's unintelligible rule explanation that sounds like a dog acquainting itself with a fire hydrant. Mike Pereira, now promoted to the NFL's vice president of officiating, admitted the next day that Morelli was applying the *wrong* rule. Morelli's attempted explanation only holds true when there is contact with an opponent, which clearly didn't happen in this case.

Four plays after the interception was unfairly taken away, Indianapolis scored and completed a 2-point conversion, making it a 3-point game.

And then things got really nutty.

The Colts got the ball back, down 21-18, with just over two minutes to play. But after three plays that went nowhere, Manning was sacked on fourth down, back at his own 2. Game over, again. Right? Wrong.

Jerome Bettis, who hadn't lost a fumble in more than 450 carries, coughed it up as he was going in for the clinching touchdown. And if not for an improbable game-saving tackle by quarterback Ben Roethlisberger, safety Nick Harper would have returned that fumble for a game-winning touchdown the other way.

As it was, Harper's return gave Indy new life in the final

Super Bowl XL, Seahawks vs. Steelers: Even though Ben Roethlisberger comes up just short of the goal line, the referees ruled the play a Pittsburgh second quarter touchdown.

minute, and a chance at a field goal to send things into overtime. But with just 17 seconds left on the clock, the normally sure-footed Mike Vanderjagt was wide right from 46 yards.

As they should have, Pittsburgh prevailed through the frenzied finish. And as he should have been, referee Pete Morelli was properly castigated in the press.

Steel City Steal

February 5, 2006: Super Bowl XL, Steelers vs. Seahawks

Not to take anything away from the Steelers' fifth Super Bowl title—they won three playoff games on the road and became the first-ever sixth seed to advance to the Super Bowl. But if we're being honest, this Lombardi Trophy was delivered to them on a silver platter by the game's referees.

Seattle and Pittsburgh took very different paths during the 2005 season. The Seahawks, led by record-setting MVP Shaun Alexander, were the class of the NFC from start to finish, at one point ripping off eleven straight wins. The Steelers suffered a three-game losing streak as late as December and faced a final Sunday must-win to even make the playoffs.

But after rattling off playoff road victories in Cincinnati, Indianapolis, and Denver, sixth-seeded Pittsburgh rolled into the Super Bowl as the favorite.

Both teams spent most of the first quarter shaking off the jitters. The game started with four straight punts, including a pair of 3-and-outs by the Steelers. But finally the Seahawks were able to mount a drive, and after a pair of Matt Hasselbeck completions put the ball at the Pittsburgh 16, Hasselbeck hit Darrell Jackson for the game's first score.

Or shall we say, apparent score. Back judge Bob Waggoner, late and only after Pittsburgh's Chris Hope began to make the call himself, threw a flag for offensive pass interference.

Both players were hand-checking for position, and at best the contact was a touch foul that should have gone uncalled. But for the Seahawks, the penalty turned their first touchdown into a field goal.

The score stayed like that, 3-0, until late in the second quarter when, on 3rd-and-goal, Ben Roethlisberger appeared to land just short of the end zone. Head linesman Mark Hittner ran in from the sideline, holding up his upfield arm as if to spot the ball. But then suddenly, and only after Roethlisberger reached the ball across the goal line, Hittner raised his other arm to signal touchdown.

Instead of facing a 4th-and-goal in the half's closing minute, and having to choose between a field goal attempt or a fourth-down gamble, Pittsburgh had its touchdown and a 7-3 halftime lead.

Fast forward now to the fourth quarter where the Steelers were clinging to a precarious 14-10 lead. After starting back at their own 2-yard line, Seattle drove all the way to the Pittsburgh 19. And following an 18-yard pass across the middle to tight end Jerramy Stevens, the Seahawks were one yard away from completing a 98-yard lead- and momentum-taking touchdown drive.

At least that would have been the situation, had referee Bill Leavy not called a backbreaking phantom holding penalty on right tackle Sean Locklear. By all angles the replay shows that Locklear's block against linebacker Clark Haggans was legal. But only one angle mattered, and it belonged to Leavy.

Three plays later, and with the ball now back on the Steelers 34 after the holding penalty and a sack, Hasselbeck threw an interception to Ike Taylor. And then, even more bizarrely, Hasselbeck was subsequently flagged 15 yards for illegally "blocking" Taylor as he tried to make the tackle.

While yes, it is illegal to tackle a blocker, which is what the refs penalized Hasselbeck for, it has never been illegal to tackle the man with the football, which is what Hasselbeck actually did.

It was a strange and by no means insignificant call that was never fully explained.

Four plays later, and with the aid of the bonus 15 yards, Pittsburgh put the game out of reach with a 43-yard touchdown pass to Hines Ward.

Everyone had an opinion immediately following the game, and the vast majority of them outside the Steelers' locker room were negative. Columnists and talk show hosts across the country called the refs' efforts "pathetic," claiming that Bill Leavy and his crew "robbed the Seahawks" and "ruined Super Bowl XL."

Seahawks head coach Mike Holmgren got into the criticism act during an after-game rally back in Seattle. The normally diplomatic Holmgren said, "We knew it was going to be tough playing against the Steelers. But I didn't know we were going to have to take on the guys in striped shirts, too."

The NFL, to its credit, immediately came to the defense of Leavy—something it's been slow to do in the past. League spokesman Greg Aiello said the Super Bowl was "properly officiated," and as in most games with "tight plays," there was "some disagreement."

And in that spirit, we reserve the right to respectfully disagree with Mr. Aiello.

Whistling While You Work
November 11, 2007: Colts at Chargers

At the risk of inviting great criticism, scorn, and ridicule, we are asserting that despite the Colts special teams allowing two returns for touchdowns, missing two field goals themselves (the last one a 29-yard chip shot), and Peyton Manning's mind boggling franchise-record six interceptions (ironically coming just two weeks after breaking Johnny Unitas's career touchdown record), it was the referees that cost Indianapolis the win at San Diego in 2007.

No one can deny the pitiful performance by Indianapolis that Sunday night in Southern California as the defending Super Bowl champions. But no one can deny that the Chargers, also coming off a great 2006, out-stunk Indy on both sides of the football.

For all of Manning's problems, San Diego's Philip Rivers was even worse. The Chargers quarterback threw for a mere 104 yards with his biggest play coming when he literally dropped the football in his own endzone and watched it get covered by linebacker Gary Brackett for an Indianapolis touchdown. And even though it was Manning who was breaking new ground in turnover futility, his passer rating for the day was higher than that of Rivers'—49.4 vs. 30.6.

It should also be noted, and applauded, that the Colts defense allowed just 10 points after all of those turnovers.

Those factors taken by themselves should have, and would have, been enough for the Colts to escape the San Diego rain with a win. Good teams find ways to win when they play terrible games. But the reason Indianapolis flew home on the short end of the nationally televised affair was because, even though they overcame their own shortcomings, they couldn't climb past the referee's.

It was late in the first quarter and the Chargers were already up, 16-0, when Rivers threw one of his two interceptions to Clint Sessions. But as the Colts linebacker took the pick from his own endzone, all the way to the San Diego 10-yard line, the referees called the play dead because of an inadvertent whistle. Instead of knocking on the door of their first touchdown of the game, Indianapolis was given a touchback, effectively wiping out 70 yards of field position.

Inadvertent whistles do happen. And to a degree we can forgive that, even if Colts general manager Bill Pollian cannot. When Pollian was asked about the inadvertent whistle the week following the loss, he responded, "The last time I saw one was in Pop Warner, and that's where they belong."

But what makes this whistle much harder to forgive is the admission on the NFL Network's *Total Access* by the league's head of officials, Mike Pereira, that the referee in question was new to the NFL in 2007 and had simply forgotten that the rule on when a player is down is different than it is in college.

He forgot?

If he is having a hard time remembering all of the rules in the NFL, then perhaps he shouldn't be paid to enforce said rules. It's as Jerry Glanville was famously overheard saying on NFL Films: "This is the NFL, which stands for 'not for long' if you keep making calls like that."

In fact, the problem may lie in the very use of the word

"inadvertent." *The American Heritage Dictionary* defines inadvertent as, "Not duly attentive. Marked by unintentional lack of care." It then directs us to the word "careless" for all relative synonyms.

An NFL official should be nothing if not attentive. And great care should be taken any time they make a ruling that can change a game's final outcome. As happened twice more in the fourth quarter.

We feel that the inadvertent point-robbing whistle in the first quarter was the game's biggest grievance. But Indianapolis was much more outraged by two calls in the Colts second-to-last possession that ultimately ended their comeback.

Driving for the game-winning score while simultaneously attempting to run out the clock, Indianapolis appeared to pick up a first down at the Chargers six-yard line that would accomplish both goals. But a booth challenge overruled the ball spot, and Indy instead was faced with a 4th-and-one from the seven. In the words of Bill Pollian, "We assumed that Joseph Addai made the first down. So did everyone else in America. Unfortunately one guy in the building didn't."

Indianapolis then did what football teams have been doing since man first discovered fire. They lined up on fourth down and tried to draw the defense offsides. But after a few hard counts and some abrupt, but legal, motion—also taken straight out of *Football Coaching for Dummies*—it was Indianapolis that drew a flag. The penalty: simulating a snap.

Of course they were simulating a snap. They were trying to draw the defense offsides. But the Colts only had players moving that were allowed to move. And only in directions that they were allowed to go. If simulating a snap is now illegal, then anytime a quarterback says "hike," but the ball isn't actually snapped by the center, a flag has to be thrown.

At the time it seemed like a bizarre and wrong call, but also insignificant. Instead of a 24-yard field goal to win the game, Mr.

Clutch, Adam Vinatieri, was facing an equally easy 29-yarder. It was good before he even kicked it.

But it wasn't. Vinatieri's game-winning kick faded to the right and failed to save Manning and the Colts by just inches—inches that would have been moot had he been kicking from five yards closer.

Football is played on a 360' x 160' field. But it is forever a game of inches. And thus, there is no such thing as an insignificant call.

Your calls had better be Super Bowl calls . . . We don't want to determine the outcome of a game unless it's the most blatant thing you've seen.

—JERRY SEEMAN
NFL REFEREE (1975–1991)

Officials are the only guys who can rob you then get a police escort out of the stadium.

—RON BOLTON
FORMER NFL DEFENSIVE BACK

I occasionally get birthday cards from fans. But it's often the same message: They hope it's my last.

—AL FORMAN
FORMER NATIONAL LEAGUE UMPIRE

COLLEGE FOOTBALL

pending a gameday Saturday afternoon on a college campus
is one of those uniquely American experiences. Which
is ironic, considering the sport of football, that for so many
Americans defines their six or seven sometimes hazy years as a
college undergrad, can trace its roots back to an English soccer
player who got fed up with only using his feet. (Which leaves
one to wonder just how much innovation is jump-started by the
inspiration of irritation.)

It was that unhappy Brit that begat rugby, which begat
American rugby, which begat American football—played initially
with twenty-five-man sides—which, beginning in 1880, was
modified by Yale player Walter Camp into the game we know
today, sort of. Field goals were worth 5 points, touchdowns were
worth 4, passing was illegal, and death was fairly common. In
1905 alone eighteen players were killed in games.

The public's outcry at the barbarity of the sport, and
President Theodore Roosevelt's threat that if the game wasn't
made safer, he'd pressure Congress to make playing football
a federal crime (seriously), thankfully led to further rules

changes, including a neutral zone, scrimmage lines and the requirement that six men line up on them, and the outlawing of the deadly "flying wedge" and other carnage-creating interlocking formations.

Now today's civilized college football fan prefers that death come only to the men wearing stripes and carrying whistles.

Fifth Down

October 6, 1990: Colorado at Missouri

In their three hundred years of combined academia, the Universities of Colorado and Missouri have turned out Nobel laureates, NASA astronauts, and Supreme Court justices. These two institutions of higher learning boast the revolutionary minds of Sam Walton (MU), founder of Wal-Mart; Trey Parker and Matt Stone (CU), co-creators of *South Park*; Sheryl Crow (MU), of songwriting and multiple Grammy-winning fame; and by far the brightest thinker of them all, James Barton (CU), the co-founder of TiVo. (Please contact your local post office and join our petition for the *James Barton: American Hero* stamp.)

It is ironic then, that amidst the respected social commentators, ground-breaking mathematicians, and pillars of business and law, on an October Saturday in 1990 these two schools had their fates cast by a crew of officials who couldn't count to four.

Even without the infamous ending that today leaves those in attendance (including one of us) still scratching their heads, it was a great game. Having just come off a win at Arizona State, the overmatched and unranked Missouri Tigers displayed an uncharacteristic confidence in their battle with No. 12 Colorado. Mizzou's vertical passing game, led by the strong arm of quarterback Kent Kiefer, was deadly, converting on a pair of long touchdown passes that kept pace with Eric Bieniemy, Mike Pritchard, and the Colorado Buffaloes' workmanlike option attack. And as the game reached the critical final drive, it was Missouri on top, 31-27.

Following a long completion by Colorado that gave the Buffs a 1st-and-goal at the 4-yard line with just 30 seconds to play, quarterback Charles Johnson (playing for the injured Darian Hagan) spiked the ball to stop the clock. On second down a handoff to Bieniemy carried the ball to the 1, and with 18 seconds left Colorado used its final timeout. On third down, and after huddling up with head coach Bill McCartney and offensive coordinator Gary Barnett, Johnson again handed the ball to Bieniemy, who again failed to cross the goal line.

The scramble was on to get everyone untangled for the final play. The clock was ticking and Colorado had no timeouts. And after referees stopped the countdown at 8 seconds because Missouri was taking too long to unpile, and then quickly restarted it, the two teams lined up for fourth down. Johnson took the snap . . . dropped back one step . . . and then, with 2 seconds left, he spiked the ball. What the__?!!?

It was the fourth play of the series, but the down marker read "3," and in the ensuing and confusing final few seconds, and on what was now fifth down, Colorado scored the game-winning touchdown, although replays and a color photo on the front page of the *Columbia Daily Tribune* showed that Johnson's quarterback keeper actually came up short, and was only called a touchdown after he slithered into the end zone on his back after he was down.

It seems impossible, or certainly improbable, that a crew of seven game officials, led by referee J. C. Louderback, and two complete coaching staffs could lose track of a count to four. But here is how it happened. After Colorado ran its second-down play (the first Bieniemy handoff) and called timeout, the official manning the down marker forgot to advance it forward. So when the Buffs broke the huddle to run third down, "officially" it was still second down, for a second time.

As the referee, J. C. Louderback should have also been

keeping track of the downs the way all football referees do—a rubber band looped around the corresponding number of fingers. But why he failed to catch the double second downs, despite his finger failsafe, has never been fully explained. It's likely that Louderback was afflicted with the same self-doubt that prevented anyone on the Missouri sideline from raising the red flag—a presumption that the down marker *must* be right, and therefore they were wrong.

The seven offending officials were immediately suspended by the Big 8 conference, but the request by Missouri chancellor Haskell Monroe to cancel Colorado's 33-31 victory and have the Tigers declared the winner was denied. Big 8 commissioner Carl James said in a statement, "It has been determined that, in accordance with the football playing rules, the allowance of the fifth down is not a correctable error. The final score in the Colorado-Missouri football game will remain as posted."

In the days and weeks that followed the game, Colorado coach Bill McCartney refused to acknowledge his team's undeserved fortune, focusing instead on Missouri's slippery field. And his continued denials of the dispensation clearly had the desired effect. In January, after Colorado beat Notre Dame in the Orange Bowl (see Scrubbed Rocket Launch), America's sportswriters awarded Colorado the college football national championship—albeit with an asterisk the size of Pike's Peak.

Fifth Down—The Early Years
November 16, 1940: Cornell at Dartmouth

There was a time in this country when college football was not governed by television networks, money-hungry athletic directors, championship-demanding alumni, and coaches who go about recruiting willfully ignorant of character. It was an age when integrity, fair play, and unclouded competition were more important than national rankings and bowl wins. An era of Saturday afternoons that were about shaping and improving the futures of young men, instead of lining the pockets of the NCAA.

The time was 1940.

The king of college football during America's final year of blissful isolationist ignorance (that ended December 7, 1941) was Ivy League power Cornell. The Big Red was coming off an undefeated national championship season in 1939 and riding a gaudy 17-game win streak when it made the November trip to Hanover, New Hampshire, to face rival Dartmouth. The inferior Big Green (even nicknames reflected the simpler time) had already lost four games in 1940 and was a cinch to drop a fifth, underdogs by more than two touchdowns.

The action that afternoon failed to follow form. Dartmouth, having lost to Cornell 35-6 the year before, had prepared all fall for their rivals from Ithaca, New York, and played the No. 1–ranked Big Red to a first half 0-0 draw. The Green then took the lead in the fourth quarter on a Bob Krieger 27-yard field goal, and with snow now falling, Cornell's win streak and possible repeat national championship seemed to be slipping away.

Cornell, however, would not go quietly, taking the ball from its own 48 and driving it to the Dartmouth goal line in the final 1:30 of play. But on fourth down and just inches from the come-from-behind victory, the Big Red was called for delay of game following a timeout. That penalty pushed the ball back to the 5-yard line for Cornell's final play, an end zone pass from Walt Scholl to Bill Murphy that was broken up at the last second by Dartmouth's Don Norton, appearing to preserve the upset win.

"I would have intercepted it, but I knew it was fourth down," remembered Norton.

But as the Dartmouth bench celebrated and their players moved to their offensive positions, prepared to run out the final two seconds, referee Red Friesell set the ball up for another

Cornell play. Muted protests from Dartmouth (referees were too respected to yell at) followed, and head linesman Joe McKinney challenged Friesell's ruling. But the respected referee held firm, noting that the scoreboard down marker read only "3."

Cornell would get its extra play, and this time, now on fifth down, Scholl's pass to Murphy in the end zone was completed for the touchdown. The Big Red had escaped Hanover with a 7-3 win.

On the train ride home some of the Cornell players and coaches began to hear whispers of a "bonus" fifth down, but brushed it off as confusion over the penalty they'd received in the closing seconds. However, on Sunday, after the game film had been developed, Cornell was faced with the incontrovertible motion picture evidence that they had in fact stolen a victory that Dartmouth deserved.

Head coach Carl Snavely called a team meeting to inform his players of the mistake in their favor, leaving the ultimate decision on what to do up to them, but suggesting, "Let's be good sports and give it back."

In an almost unanimous vote the players agreed with their coach, prompting Cornell to send this message by telegram to Dartmouth the following day: "We relinquish our claim to the victory and extend our congratulations to Dartmouth."

Dartmouth athletic director William McCarter responded: "Thank you for your wire. Dartmouth accepts the victory and your congratulations and salutes the Cornell team, the honored and honorable opponent of her longest unbroken football rivalry."

Cornell's voluntary forfeit ended its win streak, stripped away its top ranking, and destroyed its hopes for a repeat national championship. But as Cornell senior captain Walter Matuszak explained, "It was a matter of conscience. It was the right thing to do."

1940 was indeed a different time.

Catholics vs. Convicts

October 15, 1988: Miami at Notre Dame

An enterprising Notre Dame student armed with a knack for alliteration and a gross of heat-transfer iron-ons dubbed the 1988 clash between his beloved Fighting Irish and the hated Miami Hurricanes "Catholics vs. Convicts." And in the process of making a tidy profit on T-shirt sales in the South Bend area, he also nicknamed one of the great rivalries in college football.

On the field, prior to 1988, there wasn't much give and take. In 1985, Miami showed Irish coach Gerry Faust the door at Notre Dame with a 58-7 thumping at the Orange Bowl. And in 1987, on its way to the national championship, Miami shut out Lou Holtz and the Irish 24-0 in South Bend. The only place where the 'Canes didn't look superior was in the papers. A number of players appeared on Miami's police blotter; longtime Hurricane booster and member of the rap group 2 Live Crew, Luther Campbell, was said to have been paying players cash bonuses for good plays on the field; and a former academic advisor at the university admitted to helping more than fifty football players falsify Pell Grant applications.

Hurricanes quarterback Steve Walsh, however, pointed out before the game in 1988 that Miami had in fact more Catholics on its roster than Notre Dame, including himself and his entire offensive line. But "Catholics vs. Other Catholics of Questionable Character" wasn't considered apparel worthy.

The game, remembered as much for its pregame fight between the two teams in the tunnel as it was for the great on-field play, was a classic battle, punctuated by an incredible and controversial fourth quarter. With Miami trailing 31-24 late in the game, and in danger of losing its 36-game win streak, Walsh hit running back Cleveland Gary for an apparent fourth-down game-tying touchdown. The ball popped free shortly *after* Gary crossed the goal line for the score—a fact supported by every television replay—but the officials erroneously ruled it a fumble, ending Miami's chance and giving possession over to the Irish at their own 20-yard line.

Miami did eventually get the ball back and score what could have been a game-tying touchdown in the final minute. But Hurricane head coach Jimmy Johnson made the now infamous and failed decision to go for 2 (this was before the days of overtime), which allowed Notre Dame to prevail, 31-30. Of course, Johnson's gamble would have been rendered moot had Gary's touchdown catch counted, as it should have.

With the aid of the win over No. 1 Miami, coming with the assistance of the officials, Notre Dame went on to finish the regular season 12-0. The Irish then beat West Virginia in the Fiesta Bowl to capture their first national championship since 1977. Miami also didn't lose another game, beating Nebraska in the Orange Bowl and finishing one unfair spot behind Notre Dame in the polls.

No one ever claimed that "the luck of the Irish" was just or fair.

Buckeye Desert Boon
January 3, 2003: Fiesta Bowl, Ohio State vs. Miami

College football's Bowl Championship Series (BCS) has taken more than its fair share of criticism over the years, and much of it largely deserved. In 1998, in its first year in existence, Kansas State, finishing No. 3 in the final BCS standings, was passed over for a BCS bowl in favor of Ohio State (No. 4) and Florida (No. 8). That prompted the "Kansas State Rule," a guarantee that each of the top four teams would get a bid—which ironically the very next season didn't protect then-No. 6 Kansas State from getting bumped for No. 8 Michigan.

There was also the Nebraska fiasco in 2001, when the Huskers

2003 Fiesta Bowl, Miami vs. Ohio State: Miami's Glenn Sharpe is called for pass interference, giving the Buckeyes new life, and ultimately the national championship.

lost to Colorado 62-36 to end the regular season—costing them a spot in the Big XII Championship Game—but still managed to secure a date in the national championship game, edging out . . . Colorado. Following the 2003 season, five teams with one loss each found themselves vying for just two championship spots (Oklahoma and LSU got them). And in 2004 both Utah and Auburn finished the season unbeaten, including wins in BCS bowls, but never had a chance to play for the national championship.

But not wanting to lose our objectivity in regard to the B.S. BCS—which ranks somewhere between New Coke and Capri pants for men on the master list of the world's bad ideas—we would also like to acknowledge some of the standout games it has given us, with the 2003 Fiesta Bowl between Miami and Ohio State topping the list.

And as significant as this game was in the historically rich tapestry of college athletics, it was also not without controversy.

To be fair to Ohio State, they did legitimately go toe-to-toe with the faster, stronger, and better Hurricanes. The Buckeyes never trailed by more than 7 points, and led by as much as 10 in the second half, before Miami tied it with a 40-yard field goal on the final play of the fourth quarter.

On the opening possession of the first overtime, Miami scored on a 7-yard pass from Ken Dorsey to Kellen Winslow Jr., putting the 'Canes a defensive stop away from claiming their sixth national title in twenty years. And when Glenn Sharpe broke up a pass in the end zone on fourth down of Ohio State's possession, it looked like the $30,000 Waterford Crystal trophy was headed back to South Florida.

"I'm there on the bench, head down, about in tears," recalled Ohio State cornerback Dustin Fox. "I saw [Ohio State quarterback] Craig Krenzel sitting down on the 20-yard line like things were over. Then I looked up and the screen says, 'Marker Down.'"

The marker had been thrown for pass interference on Sharpe, and to call it "controversial" is to call the series of 200-foot Tostitos advertisements that adorned Sun Devil Stadium "mildly overbearing."

The line judge, who was just feet from the play, made no move for his flag, obviously ruling the pass incomplete. Several photographers, reporters, and cameramen assumed that was the call, running out onto the field to capture the Miami celebration. But field judge Terry Porter, after reaching for his flag, then hesitating, finally made the decision to complete the history-changing call.

Instead of game over and a Miami Hurricanes repeat national championship, quarterback Craig Krenzel tied the game with a 1-yard plunge on the very next play. And following Maurice Clarett's touchdown run to begin the second overtime, Ohio State got the defensive stop that ended Miami's perfect season and gave the 11½ point underdog Buckeyes a 31-24 win and their first national championship since 1968.

"You hate for an official to make that call," Miami coach Larry Coker said in his postgame press conference. "The loss was, without question, devastating."

Military Time
December 7, 1963: Army vs. Navy

On November 22, 1963, the United States suffered an agonizing wound to its heart. No single day in the last sixty years of American history, outside of 9/11, shook this nation more. It was the day that President John F. Kennedy was suddenly taken by a sniper's bullet, felling an entire country in the process.

As with most sporting events taking place in the wake of the assassination of the young president, the Army-Navy game was postponed indefinitely. And only after the grieving Kennedy family issued a specific request that the game be played was it rescheduled for the fittingly consecrated date of December 7.

There are few sights in sports more stirring than the pregame march of the Corps of Cadets and the Brigade of Midshipmen. It begins the annual Army-Navy tradition with a reminder that for these men and women, future commissioned officers who will one day work side by side in defense of our nation, football is secondary. And on this date, in honor of the slain President, the flawless march to midfield was accompanied by a color guard and followed by a reverberating moment of silence that was heard around the world.

Then it was time for football.

Led by Mr. All-American Heisman-Trophy-winner Roger

Staubach, No. 2 Navy played its way to what looked to be an insurmountable 21-7 lead. But Army had its own secret-weapon quarterback, Rollie Stichweh—a two-way player who also doubled as a defensive back—and with six minutes to play, the junior quarterback scored from one yard out.

The touchdown, and subsequent 2-point conversion, did more than just bring Army to within 6 points of the lead. At the instruction of CBS television director Tony Verna, a former Cadet himself who at age twenty-nine was about to revolutionize television in a way as significant as James Barton's TiVo, Stichweh's score was shown to the audience again. It was the first use of television replay in a sporting event, ever.

Stichweh, however, was too busy trying to beat Navy to worry about his future place on the back of a Trivial Pursuit card. And when Army tried an onside kick, the man who was doing his best to upstage Staubach that December Saturday afternoon made the recovery. He then drove Army to the Navy 2-yard line with just 20 seconds to play.

With the game in the balance and just seconds left, Stichweh broke the Army huddle. But as the Cadets got set at the line of scrimmage, the crowd noise became deafening, and Stichweh was forced to step away from under center and ask the refs to quiet the crowd. They obliged him by stopping the clock, but just as Army was returning to its huddle to reset the call, the referees, without warning, restarted the clock. And by the time Stichweh and the Cadets realized what had happened, it was too late. Time had run out.

The Middies escaped Philadelphia with the 21-15 win, beating Army for the fifth year in a row. And the following year, still feeling the scar of the tragedy that played out in Dallas, the annual site of the game, Municipal Stadium in Philadelphia, was renamed for the fallen commander in chief.

THE Rivalry
November 24, 1973: Ohio State at Michigan

Reliable legend has it that while returning from a recruiting trip to Michigan, an assistant coach for Ohio State's Woody Hayes noticed that the car they were driving was running low on gas. As he began to pull off the road to find a filling station, Hayes insisted that he get back on the highway and keep driving to Ohio. A few more minutes passed, and with the needle continuing to drop, again the assistant coach told Hayes that they needed to fuel up.

The second suggestion was simply too much for Hayes, who flew into one of his trademark tirades, "No goddammit, you will not pull in and fill up! I will not buy one goddamn drop of gas in the state of Michigan! We'll push this goddamn car to the Ohio line before I give this state one nickel of my money!"

Luckily for everyone on the trip, the car just made it, coasting on fumes into the first gas station across the state line.

Whether or not this story is true, or has been embellished over the years, is beside the point. Woody Hayes's hatred for Michigan was pure and complete, and if he had ever really found himself in need of gas while in "that state up north"—the only way Hayes would refer to Michigan—he no doubt would have risked running out to avoid giving them his commerce.

It's the kind of hatred that makes this an indefinable college football rivalry in comparison to all the rest. It exists in a category all its own. Sometimes these seeds of resentment are attributed to an 1835 conflict over ownership of a stretch of land known as the Toledo Strip that nearly erupted into a Michigan-Ohio civil war. But probably the rivalry simply finds its roots in the annual gridiron war that's been waging for more than a century, claiming casualties along the way.

The most famous of these pigskin hostilities happened in 1973, the same year the U.S. Supreme Court finally settled the Toledo Strip border issue and the two states' competing claims for the waters of Lake Erie, ultimately taking half of Michigan's Turtle Island and handing it over to Ohio.

It would not be the only gift given to the Buckeye state that year.

"The Game" in Ann Arbor in 1973 was set up to be a classic even before kickoff. It was Woody Hayes vs. Bo Schembechler; No. 1 Ohio State (10-0) vs. No. 4 Michigan (10-0); and the largest crowd to date to ever see a regular season college football game, an announced attendance of 105,223.

The game ended in a bitterly fought 10-10 tie, and amazingly absent any controversy. But those sixty minutes of football stalemate left the two rivals also in a tie for the Big Ten title, which left the conference with a rather murky Rose Bowl picture that needed to be cleared up by a vote among the conference's athletic directors. For years the conference had a "no repeat rule" regarding bids to the Rose Bowl, and even though the rule was no longer officially on the books, precedent dictated that since Ohio State had been to Pasadena the season before, this year it would be newly crowned cochampion Michigan.

"We knew we had to win this one to go [to the Rose Bowl]," said Hayes in his postgame press conference, echoing the expectations of everyone else in Ann Arbor that Saturday.

One factor that these assumptions didn't consider was the broken collarbone suffered in the game by Michigan quarterback Dennis Franklin. The athletic directors, however, did. And fearful that a second-team quarterback wouldn't be able to compete with USC in the Rose Bowl, Ohio State was given a second straight trip to Pasadena by a vote of 6-4.

Even more astonishingly, one of the votes against Michigan came from Michigan State Athletic Director, and Ann Arbor graduate, Burt Smith. Smith's vote against his alma mater so incensed the state's population, according to then Michigan Athletic Director Don Canham, that Smith "eventually lost his job because of it."

As the Big Ten's lone bowl representative—that was the conference rule in 1973—Ohio State beat USC on New Year's Day by three touchdowns, finishing its season 11-0-1. And Michigan, having outscored its opponents 330-68 during an unbeaten 10-0-1 season, was forced to stay home.

Seconds to None

January 1, 1998: Rose Bowl, Michigan vs. Washington State

Remember back to the time when Washington State's Ryan Leaf was a Heisman Trophy finalist, a can't-miss NFL prospect with future All-Pro written all over his cannon right arm, and a humble team leader. Shortly after the Cougars' loss to Michigan at the Rose Bowl, Leaf attributed the offense's trouble scoring to the absence of running back Michael Black, saying, "When you lose your best player, it's tough to win games, and he is our best offensive player."

Does anyone remember *that* Ryan Leaf? Anyone? Bueller?

In fact, the twenty-one-year-old quarterback, whom Washington State coach Mike Price called "a tremendous individual," had such a solid head on his shoulders, he refused to blame an official's mistake in the closing seconds for costing the Cougars in Pasadena—a magnanimous position of palliation that the rest of his team didn't share. And neither do we.

Michigan came into New Year's Day 1998 unbeaten and looking to finish the season as the nation's No. 1 team. Washington State, on the other hand, had no national championship aspirations but was anxious to prove that in the battle of quarterback Ryan Leaf (third in the '97 Heisman balloting) vs. Charles Woodson (the '97 Heisman winner), they had the better man. (An issue that remained unresolved at the end of 1998's opening day, but has since been answered emphatically.)

Woodson scored the first point of the day when he picked off

Leaf in the end zone, preventing a first half WSU touchdown. But the junior quarterback evened things up by orchestrating a 99-yard second-half touchdown drive to give the Cougars the lead. In the fourth quarter, after Michigan had taken a 5-point lead and eaten up most of the remaining time, Leaf nearly became a legend.

Beginning possession at his own 7-yard line with no timeouts and just 29 seconds remaining, the situation for Leaf and the Cougars seemed hopeless. And after a pair of incomplete passes ran the clock down to 16 seconds, the game was all but over. Then, miraculously Leaf completed a 46-yard bomb to James Taylor at the Michigan 47-yard line, leaving 9 seconds left. Then another pass and lateral took the ball down to the Michigan 26, the clock stopping at 2 seconds as the officials moved the chains.

As the Cougars ran down the field and lined up in desperation, Leaf made plans to spike the ball as soon as the play was set, allowing his team to settle for a moment before their one remaining chance. But as the ref blew the whistle and Leaf took the snap and spiked the ball, the clock never stopped, running all the way to double zeros. Michigan had survived and preserved its perfect record.

"When we ran onto the field [to celebrate], I wasn't sure what was going to happen," Michigan head coach Lloyd Carr said. "I was hoping that if there was any doubt in [the officials'] minds, they would forget about it because there would be too many people to kick off the field."

On the other sideline there was no doubt in the mind of Wazzu coach Mike Price, expressed in his curt address to the media following the game: "It shouldn't take two seconds to down the ball. We still would have had to go out there and make the play, but it would have been nice to get that chance."

Who knows what Ryan Leaf, having just taken his team 67 yards in less than 16 seconds and clearly awaiting guaranteed greatness in the NFL, could have done with that chance? But it's probably a safe bet that Michigan, which ended up sharing the national championship with Nebraska (see Foot-Ball), was just fine never finding out.

The Nick of Time

November 3, 2001: Michigan at Michigan State

In November of 2001 two things happened. Ryan Leaf, then a Cowboy, played his final NFL game, ending his unbelievably bad career—not including his much-ballyhooed foray into flag football—with fourteen touchdowns, thirty-six interceptions, and three recorded temper tantrums. And Washington State football fans finally got over getting jobbed at the Rose Bowl in the closing seconds against Michigan.

The former eventuality happened with indignant Dallas Cowboy fans asking, "*Why* did we do that?" The latter resolution resulted with Michigan Wolverine fans scratching their heads and questioning, "*How* did they do that?"

Unthinking eagerness was the answer to both queries.

Michigan took a 24-20 lead over Michigan State on a John Navarre-to-Jermaine Gonzales touchdown pass with less than 5 minutes to play. And after an exchange of punts left the Spartans with one final chance to drive for the winning score, the game appeared to be over when the bruised and battered Jeff Smoker— he was sacked twelve times—threw an incompletion on 4th-and-16 with just 1:18 to play.

But away from the harmlessly bouncing ball that seemingly sealed victory for the Wolverines, defensive back Jeremy LeSueur was called for a 15-yard, automatic-first-down facemask penalty on wide receiver Charles Rogers, giving MSU new, and as it turned out, sustainable life. The penalty put the ball at the Michigan 35, a pass to Herb Haygood moved it to the 17, and a Michigan penalty and a completion to T. J. Duckett set up the Spartans at the 3 with just 15 seconds left.

Smoker took the second-down snap from the shotgun and rolled out to his right, stopping, starting, then taking off for the end zone, only to come up short at the 2-yard line. With no timeouts left, the scattered Spartans scrambled to get back to the line as Smoker called for a clock-stopping spike. As Smoker took the snap, the clock struck :01, but after he moved one step back and spiked the ball in desperation, amazingly, the hometown clock still read :01.

On the very next, and extra play, Smoker completed a 2-yard touchdown to Duckett, giving Michigan State the upset 26-24 win and effectively ending Michigan's shot at a national championship.

"I looked up at the clock when I said 'Hut,' " Smoker explained afterward. "I believe there were two seconds still on the clock. I was pretty sure I spiked it in time."

The less-than-concrete definitives of "I believe" and "pretty sure" summed up the "we got away with one" feeling on the Michigan State sideline. And capturing the mood for the Wolverines was radio broadcaster Frank Beckmann's exclamation: "This game was stolen!"

The broken and beaten Lloyd Carr sounded less like a head coach and more like a despondent parent when he told reporters, "Our kids deserved better. I'm sure the Big Ten will do the right thing, but that won't change the outcome."

An outcome that gave Michigan State the annual Paul Bunyan Trophy, the Spartan Stadium clock operator free haircuts for life and a future in local government, and the still-bitter Washington State fans 2,100 miles away the sweet release of karmic revenge.

Count Your Blessings

September 17, 1988: Florida State at Clemson

Apologists for game-show contestants that wilt under the pressure of competition and the glare of hot lights on a sound stage tell us that ordinary knowledge can sometimes get lost in the tension of the moment. It's how a pop-cultured astrophysicist by day and Lindsay Lohan blog moderator by night can get ceremoniously dumped on *Jeopardy* by Alex Trebek's—"Sorry. We were looking for 'What is *Herbie Fully Loaded*' "—while the gaggles of us at home snigger at said genius confusing it with the critically acclaimed *Confessions of a Teenage Drama Queen*.

On a much more pedestrian level, it is this same brain cramp phenomenon that elicits catatonic stares from the trio of *Wheel of Fortune* tomfools when the puzzle board reads "*Phrase*—KEEP IT _IMPLE _TUPID."

And even more plebeian, it sometimes manifests itself in the bodies of college football referees, rendering them incapable of simple addition when surrounded by several thousand eighteen- and nineteen-year-olds who are unlocking the mysteries of the universe through complex calculus, as it did on September 17, 1988 in Clemson, South Carolina.

Florida State began the 1988 season as the No. 1 team in the country. But after a pair of up-and-down weeks that included a season-opening 31-0 thrashing at the hands of Miami and a 49-13 win over Southern Mississippi, Bobby Bowden's No. 10 Seminoles traveled to Death Valley to face 2-0 Clemson. The favored Tigers were ranked third.

For one of the few times in recent memory, a top-10 game actually *exceeded* the hype. Late in the fourth quarter, and with the score tied 14-14, Deion Sanders snapped off an eye-catching punt return for a touchdown that momentarily gave the 'Noles the lead—and the football world a glimpse of things to come. But the Florida State celebration was short-lived. Tigers quarterback Rodney Williams grabbed the momentum back by leading Clemson to a late game-tying score of its own. And after a defensive stop forced a closing minute's punt by Florida State, it appeared that Clemson would have a chance to win on the game's final possession.

Bobby Bowden, however, had other ideas, and from his own 21-yard line and with just 1:30 to play, he stunned everyone by calling a fake punt. The "puntrooskie," as it became known, worked to perfection, with future NFL star LeRoy Butler taking it 78 yards to just short of the Clemson goal line—which is where things began to break down for the officials.

The Clemson defense held firm, stopping the 'Noles' touchdown efforts on first, second, and third downs. And with the clock ticking down to less than 30 seconds, Florida State called a timeout to bring on their field goal team to win it. Problem was, however, that FSU didn't have any timeouts left, and that set off an extended and confused meeting of the minds of the men in stripes, all the while keeping the clock stopped, essentially granting the Seminoles a fourth and extra timeout.

Finally, Florida State ran its 4th-down play, now opting out of the field goal attempt (they were 0-3 on the season) and instead going for the touchdown, which they scored. But still confused, the referees called the play back, recognizing that they hadn't penalized the Seminoles for using a timeout before the touchdown run. But as the officials (who were a hodgepodge of ACC and independent referees) reset 4th down, they still failed to mark off any penalty yards, leaving the ball at its original spot.

This time—Bowden's second bite at the apple—he called on his field goal unit to win the game, which it did, converting its first kick of the season for the 24-21 Florida State victory, made possible by the mathematically challenged mucks in black-and-white stripes.

The controversy, of course, didn't go away. And Clemson coach Danny Ford, who had just seen his perfect season and quest for a national championship unfairly end, wanted answers. Ford finally got them ten days later, sort of, when ACC supervisor of officials Bradley Faircloth issued this cryptic statement: "After a review of film and a discussion with game officials, some officiating errors were made. Some of these errors were attributable to errors in judgment and probably could have been prevented by better communication."

Oh.

Foot-Ball
November 8, 1997: Nebraska at Missouri

Football games are won and lost on last-second kicks all of the time. It's the one saving grace of kickers, and the only way these undersized masters of the mismatched shoes and single-bar facemasks can earn the right to call themselves football players. So it must have been more than a little discomforting when in 1997 Nebraska wide receiver Shevin Wiggins encroached on the kicker's previously untouched cherished terrain.

Any list of college football's greatest games will somewhere in its top-10 contain the 1997 meeting between Nebraska and Missouri. And even before the infamous ending that continues to make the replay rounds, it was a great one. Missouri struck first, shoving the opening drive down No. 1 Nebraska's throat for an early 7-0 lead. The Huskers countered with a pair of Scott Frost touchdown runs, only to be answered by a Corby Jones-to-Torey Coleman TD pass, knotting things up at 14.

Ahman Green, who ended the game with 189 yards on 30 carries, scored next for Nebraska. But a Tiger field goal and a Jones-to-Brock Olivo touchdown connection put Missouri back on top, 24-21. Frost then scored again, answered closely by a 7-yard keeper from Jones. And following a Huskers field goal by Kris Brown and a Jones-to-Eddie Brooks Missouri touchdown strike, the score stood 38-31 Missouri with 1:02 to play.

Facing a 67-yard uphill climb, Frost went to work. A completion to Kenny Cheatham picked up 27 yards. A 3rd-down catch by Matt Davison moved the ball another 13. Then it was

Cheatham again, twice, taking the ball to the Missouri 12-yard line, but now just 7 seconds remained.

On the final play, called "99 double slant," Frost took the snap and first looked left . . . then right . . . then after a brief moment of hesitation, fired a bullet at the well-covered Shevin Wiggins. The soon-to-be luckiest man in the world jumped for the ball, but just as it got to him, so did a hit from nickel back Julian Jones, and with the ball bouncing away, and taking with it Nebraska's undefeated season, Wiggins began to fall helplessly backwards.

In an instinctual move of last gasp desperation, Wiggins struck at the rapidly dropping ball with the only thing that would reach it, his foot. Amazingly, he connected, the ball popped back into the air, and, like a slow-motion sequence right out of *The Matrix*, into the picture dove Davison, snatching the football just inches above the end-zone turf.

It was a touchdown catch that defied reason and defined improbable, and it was a crushing blow to Missouri.

The psychologically destroyed Tiger defense was on the field first in overtime, and Nebraska easily scored. And when the equally deflated Missouri offense finally ran out of answers, No. 1 Nebraska escaped Faurot Field with the 45-38 win.

It was without a doubt a win for the ages, brought about by the heady (footy) play by Wiggins and the fortuitous location of the sure-handed freshman Davison. But lost in the euphoria of the moment and the hoopla of the following week was one very important fact. It was illegal and should have resulted in a 15-yard penalty. A player cannot purposefully kick the ball, and the instant replay leaves little doubt that that is exactly what Wiggins did.

When asked if the kick was intentional, Wiggins replied, "No. I think it was just a natural reaction." An answer that obviously does not place it outside the understood definition of "intentional," just as holding, grabbing a face mask, and offsides often result from "natural reactions."

Told that Wiggins claimed that he didn't kick the ball on purpose, Davison laughed, and grinning from ear to ear said, "Well, I guess it was an accident."

Two months later, by no accident, the retiring Tom Osborne and Nebraska would share the national championship with Michigan.

Bayou Boost
November 4, 1972: Ole Miss at LSU

Pick your college football-covering publication, and you'll find LSU's Tiger Stadium high on its list of most-feared road sites. Alabama's immortal head coach Bear Bryant once called it the worst place to play as a visiting team because it was "like playing inside a drum." In 1988, when Tiger quarterback Tommy Hodson hit Eddie Fuller for a 4th-down game-winning score to beat Auburn in the final minutes, the eruption by the crowd actually tripped the seismographs in the university's geology department. And during a nationally televised meeting between LSU and Auburn in 2003, the ESPN crew covering the game recorded a noise level of 117 decibels—a train horn three feet away registers 120 decibels.

Yet surprisingly, with perhaps the exception of any magazine based in or around Oxford, Mississippi, not once is LSU's clock operator given credit for Tiger Stadium's imposing presence.

When Ole Miss and LSU met in Baton Rouge in 1972, it was at the height of their rivalry. Both schools were regulars in the national rankings and on the postseason bowl schedule, and every year when they met it was a war. The season before, the Rebels snuck past the Tigers 24-22, avenging a 61-17 embarrassment in 1970, Archie Manning's final season. Everyone in both states had been looking forward to November 4.

In theory the game should have been a walkover for LSU.

They were 6-0 on the season and ranked sixth in the nation. Mississippi was a struggling 4-3. But at the risk of sounding like students at the Cliché College for Coaches, games aren't played on paper. Defying convention, the oddsmakers, and the many LSU fans that were looking ahead to Alabama the following week, Ole Miss held the lead 16-10 late in the fourth quarter.

LSU quarterback Bert Jones had one final chance. And starting at his own 20 with just over three minutes to play, he delivered, carrying out a series of completions, including one on 4th down that took the ball to the Mississippi 10-yard line with just 4 seconds left. There was only time for one more play.

Taking the final snap, Jones dropped back to throw, but looking toward the end zone he misfired on the throw, and the ball fell fatally incomplete, setting off a celebration among the Ole Miss players. A celebration that was shockingly short-lived when everyone in the stadium noticed that miraculously . . .

> **mir·a·cle** - *n.* - An event that appears inexplicable
> by the laws of nature, but is really the result of a
> hometown timekeeper.

. . . the clock still had one second on it.

Desperate to compose themselves after their interrupted victory festivities, while simultaneously attempting to formulate an explanation for how LSU's final play consumed only three seconds, Ole Miss failed to stop the Tigers' extra play. This time Jones found his mark, hitting running back Brad Davis in the back of the end zone for the 17-16 win—although whether or not he had possession before being knocked out of bounds was also a subject for debate, and the source of much anger across the state of Mississippi.

Losing to a rival by way of a timekeeper who is out to prove Einstein's theory of relativity (time is not absolute) ruffled more than a few Rebel feathers. But in dealing with their pain, and finding an outlet for their angst, Ole Miss gets an A+ for creativity. The 1973 Ole Miss media guide recorded the result like this:

MISS	**16**
LSU	**10+7**

And a sign erected on the Mississippi-Louisiana state line read: "You are now entering Louisiana. Set your clocks back four seconds."

Scrubbed Rocket Launch

January 1, 1991: Orange Bowl, Notre Dame vs. Colorado

The biggest shame to come out of the 1991 Orange Bowl between Colorado and Notre Dame wasn't the Buffaloes' undeserved national championship (see Fifth Down), or the fact that Georgia Tech, which finished the season unbeaten and with a better record than Colorado, was forced to share the then-mythical title as co-champions. The greatest injustice and paramount pang was the abject larceny of Rocket Ismail's place in sports history.

Yes, he is, and forever will be, a Heisman Trophy winner—the most storied award in sports. But in the annals of subconsciously seared unremitting moments, Ismail deserves deification, instead of the discard that he often receives.

Anytime the topic of all-time great college football plays comes up for discussion, the focus is on Cal-Stanford and "The Play"; or Doug Flutie's Heisman-winning toss to beat Miami; or Kordell Stewart's 70-yard last-second heave in Ann Arbor—all incredible plays that will never wear thin through replay, but all saddled inside a regular season game relatively devoid of national importance. Stanford and California both missed the bowl season in 1982, Miami and Boston College had no impact on the 1984 national championship race, and Colorado's amazing 1994 win at Michigan happened in September, five weeks before their championship dreams ended in Lincoln, Nebraska.

Ismail's 91-yard punt return, making Colorado's talented special teams look like a group of Pop Warner rejects, happened in the closing seconds of a New Year's Day bowl to decide the NCAA Division I-A national champion. It was, however, wiped out by a subjectively ticky-tack clipping penalty, eliminating its hardcopy existence and leaving the punt return's record to nothing more than stored memory, remembered and eventually passed on by human repositories of knowledge like Montag, Granger, and the other educated castaways in Ray Bradbury's *Fahrenheit 451.*

If you saw the play, you remember it. Trailing Colorado by 1 with just under a minute to play, Rocket Ismail took the Colorado punt inside his own 10-yard line, just hoping to improve the Notre Dame field position enough to give his offense a chance. Catching the ball, Rocket immediately spotted a seam to his right, and displaying a sprinter's burst that would have curled Carl Lewis's toes, Ismail flew through the hole and past the defenders, hugging the sideline in a beeline for a once-in-a-lifetime 91-yard-punt-return Orange Bowl win.

Except . . . the referees had thrown a flag on Notre Dame's Greg Lane for clipping on a block that nine times out of ten would have been legal, and in the closing seconds of a New Year's Day bowl game with national championship implications, should always be. That call wiped out the touchdown, cancelled the "greatest clutch performer" check that Ismail was about to cash, and handed Colorado a national championship that twice it didn't earn.

When mankind rises from the ashes like the phoenix, and learns not to repeat its self-consuming mistakes of the past, we'll be there to retell the tale and rewrite the history of the great Raghib "Rocket" Ismail.

Thorny Roses

January 1, 1979: Rose Bowl, Michigan vs. USC

An old Turkish proverb observes, "Man is harder than iron, stronger than stone, and more fragile than a rose."

The Turks might as well have been talking about legendary Michigan head coach Bo Schembechler, a fiery motivator and "coach's coach" who made his mark with fundamentally fixed players that consistently out-toughed the other team for wins. But when it came to the Rose Bowl, Schembechler's stronger-than-stone .796 winning percentage at Michigan wilted in the warm Southern California sun, illustrating the words of famed American philosophers Jan and Dean, "There's nobody meaner than the little old lady from Pasadena."

Or in the case of Bo Schembechler, the Granddaddy.

The ominous way Schembechler's Rose Bowl career began should have been an omen. The night before he was due to make his debut in "The Granddaddy of Them All," Schembechler rang in the 1970 New Year by suffering a heart attack. The next day, with Schembechler stuck in a hospital bed and defensive coordinator Jim Young taking his place as temporary head coach, Michigan lost to USC 10-3.

Two years later Michigan was back in Pasadena—with a healthy Schembechler marching the sideline—but lost to Stanford on a last-second field goal. In 1977 the Wolverines again won the Big Ten title, but again lost the Rose Bowl to USC, led by Vince Evans, Ricky Bell, and Charles White—the future Heisman Trophy winner who would play a prominent part in the game two years later.

But let's not get ahead of ourselves. Before that would happen, Michigan would run its record in the Rose Bowl under Bo Schembechler to a perfect 0-4, losing to Washington and future Pro Football Hall of Famer Warren Moon on New Year's Day, 1978.

And that takes us to the opening day of 1979, and yet another Michigan-USC battle for the roses. The scoring began in the first quarter after the Trojans picked off Big Blue quarterback Rick Leach, setting themselves up for a short and sweet 16-yard touchdown drive. Michigan finally got on the board with a field goal in the second quarter, making the score 7-3, but just moments later the game took a huge turn to the Trojans and into the annals of infamy.

On a 2nd-down play at the Michigan 3-yard line, White took the handoff and drove straight through the heart of his offensive line, only to pop out on the other side minus the football. That now belonged to Wolverine linebacker Jerry Meter, who had recovered the apparent touchdown-saving fumble at his own 1-yard line. However, before Michigan got too far into its defensive stand celebration, the line judge raised his arms to signal touchdown.

"I was just laying it down in the end zone for the ref to pick it," claimed White after the game, "like I always do." Unfortunately, replays revealed White's halfhearted fib, and the possession-changing fumble that the play should have been. The ball not only clearly came out before it ever reached the goal line, White didn't appear to ever make it in, with or without the football.

The official's mistake took a 7-3 game and a colossal momentum shift over to the Michigan sideline and turned it instead into a 14-3 USC lead. It was a 7-point difference that just so happened to provide the margin of victory in the Trojans' eventual 17-10 win.

Bo Schembechler would finally win the Rose Bowl in 1981, stopping his personal Pasadena losing streak at five games. But that win did not erase the anger at injustice that still lingered inside. When the Trojans beat Notre Dame on a similarly controversial fumble in 1982, the still bitter Schembechler cracked, "USC has really perfected that play."

Replay Dismay

September 16, 2006: Oklahoma at Oregon

Even as scores of sports dreams continue to be undone by ophthalmologically challenged referees, their blindness, in the end, is forgivable. One can't help a degenerated ocular muscle or an excessively refracted cornea. It's why we all felt so bad for the *Family Guy*'s Peter Griffin when he lost his eyesight to nickel poisoning while trying to set the world record for most nickels eaten. Thank goodness he got that eye transplant from the hobo he accidentally strangled with his guide-dog's leash.

But when imbecilic stupidity clouds what is otherwise 20/20 vision to the point that the owner of said eyesight lays waste to the immovable laws of logic (as seen plainly by those of us with a functioning cerebral cortex), clemency gives way to derision.

If you saw the September 2006 game between Oklahoma and Oregon, and you own TiVo, you no doubt immediately backed up the game late in the fourth quarter so that you could see the Ducks' recovered onside kick again. To the naked eye it looked like an Oregon player touched the ball before it had traveled the necessary 10 yards, and the single camera replay from high atop Autzen Stadium, provided by your TiVo, confirmed it. Oregon, having just pulled to within 6 points on a 16-yard Dennis Dixon touchdown run with 1:12 to play, was now out of chances. With all of college football implementing instant replay for 2006, it was assumed beyond any doubt that the play would be overturned and the Sooners would leave Eugene with the important road victory.

We promise to never make that certain but wildly mistaken assumption again.

As the play went upstairs to be reviewed by replay official Gordon Riese, an Oregon native with twenty-eight years of experience as a Pac-10 official, further angles showed that not only did Oregon's Brian Paysinger touch the ball inside the magic 10-yard mark—making the play illegal—the ball was never recovered by an Oregon player. For some as-yet-to-be explained reason, the on-field officials had ruled it an Oregon recovery even though the ball was clearly secured by Oklahoma's Allen Patrick. What referee school teaches you to signal possession without actually seeing the football? The answer: none.

So now there were two very clear reasons to overturn the play and give possession to Oklahoma, as everyone, including the ABC broadcast team of Tim Brant and Dan Fouts (an Oregon grad), assumed would happen. Key word being ass-u-me.

When the final decision was handed down from on high, referee Dave Cutaia announced to the very anxious Oregon crowd, "After review, there is conclusive evidence that the receiving team touched the ball, therefore making it live."

What? Conclusive? In the words of Dan Fouts, "Horrible call. The Ducks get an incredible break."

A shocking break that dismissed everything we've always known about the onside kick. Yes, the ball did touch an Oklahoma player. In fact, the final player to touch it was a Sooner. But BEFORE it got close enough for a member of the receiving team to get his hands on it, the ball was touched by Oregon. And in every division of football, from peewee to the pros, that's against the rules.

In defense of Riese, the replay official who says he never felt the kind of pressure on the field that he has in the replay booth, the NCAA's system of instant replay is vastly inferior to the NFL's by not giving officials in the booth the technology to freeze frames—something that's been available in the average home since the first VCR. But in reality, it's a mild defense at best. He still should have been able to see the play in live motion as the rest of us did.

Two plays after that buffoonery, the crew of officials added insult to injury when they flagged Oklahoma for pass interference on a pass that was tipped at the line of scrimmage—again in clear contrast to a well-known and often-implemented section of the rule book. And again, after the play went upstairs for review, the definitive ruling came down incorrectly in favor of Oregon.

On the very next play Oregon scored the winning touchdown.

Needless to say, the reaction from Oklahoma in the wake of the Sooners' 34-33 loss was swift, pointed, and not entirely level headed. Head coach Bob Stoops said, "They had an opportunity to get it right, and they chose not to. So I find it absolutely inexcusable and unacceptable—in particular—[that] people who had an opportunity to review it all and get it right chose not to."

Oklahoma president David Boren took the unprecedented step of sending a letter to Big 12 commissioner Kevin Weiberg, asking that his office "launch a vigorous effort to correct the situation." This in Boren's mind meant having the final result vacated from the record book.

Boren went on to say, "To describe the lapses in accurate officiating at the Oklahoma-Oregon football game last Saturday as constituting an outrageous injustice is an understatement."

"Outrageous injustice" might also be a descriptor used for the death threats that Riese received from Oklahoma fans in the days following his mistake. While we are strong advocates of ridicule, threatening an official, his wife, and his kids is just a wee bit past the line of sports sanity.

For its part, the Pac-10 did what it could to make things right. "Errors clearly were made and not corrected," said commissioner Tom Hansen. "And for that we apologize to the University of Oklahoma, coach Bob Stoops, and his players."

Coupled with the conference's apology was a one-week suspension of the officiating crew. Riese, in the wake of the death threats and what he called "skyrocketing blood pressure," asked for, and was granted, a year-long leave of absence.

And finally, because heaping servings of all-you-can-eat stupid never run low, the sportswriters who cast their votes for the AP's top-25—and had all seen the officiating travesty that stole certain victory from Oklahoma—dropped the Sooners from #15 to #17 while moving Oregon up five spots to #13.

In the words of Coach Stoops, "Truly, there can be no amends."

Our greatest fear is that we're a step away from a referee being physically assaulted. That's where we are. That's the environment that's being created.

—LAMELL McMORRIS
NATIONAL BASKETBALL REFEREES
ASSOCIATION

We're supposed to be perfect our first day on the job and show constant improvement.

—ED VARGO
NATIONAL LEAGUE umpire (1960–1983)

Judges are supposed to be unbiased, and if you believe that I have a bridge to sell you.

—DEBI THOMAS
1988 OLYMPIC bronze medal figure skater

THE OLYMPIC GAMES

The Olympic Games began in 776 BC with a simple footrace to honor the larger-than-life figure of the day, Zeus. And even though the modern games, revived in 1896 by Baron Pierre de Coubertin, don't feature the supreme ruler of the Pantheon of gods, they have given us the best mortal man has to offer in the persons of Jesse Owens, Mark Spitz, Eric Heiden, and Nadia Comaneci.

The Olympic Games are defined by moments of greatness—Bob Beamon soaring 29 feet, 2½ inches in Mexico City, Mike Eruzione scoring the game-winning goal against the Soviet Union in Lake Placid, and Mary Lou Retton sticking her final vault to win gymnastics' all-around title in Los Angeles.

But unfortunately these games that were once powerful enough to stop warfare, and all these centuries later still inspire the achievements of young amateur athletes in every corner of the globe, have often been the stage for controversy and calculated criminality.

Five different Olympics (1956, '76, '80, '84, and '88) have suffered because of large national boycotts; several more

Games have barred athletes, teams, and entire countries from participation; and in virtually every Olympic Games in the modern era, gold medals have been decided by incompetence, arrogance, politics, and the thing George Washington said "few men have the virtue to withstand"—bribes.

Britain's Golden Rule

London 1908: Men's Track and Field 400-meter Finals

Following the disastrous Olympics of 1900 and 1904, in which the Games lasted for more than four months, were badly organized, and held alongside and largely overshadowed by the more popular World's Fair, it was no longer a question of if but when Pierre de Coubertin's international athletic creation would breathe its final breath.

Then in 1906, almost as if the ancient Greek god Zeus himself, from some centuries-old resting place in the center of the Earth, was trying to breathe new life into the Games that were once held in his honor, Mt. Vesuvius blew its top.

Italy, burdened with relief and rebuilding costs, and facing an economic crisis, was forced to cancel its already shaky 1908 Olympic bid. London took over, quickly built a 68,000-seat stadium that was seen at the time as a technological marvel, and then held a successful and organized Games that produced innovations and historical achievements. And many of the most familiar aspects of today's Olympics can trace their lineage back to London.

For the first time, qualifying standards and preliminary rounds were used. The British built the first ever "Olympic-sized" pool, and clearly marked it into lanes. And the marathon, previously a race of twenty-five miles, was lengthened to twenty-six so that it could begin in front of Windsor Castle.

That distance was extended even farther when the finish line was moved to accommodate the royal box, and the start line, at the request of Princess Mary, was moved onto Castle grounds and beneath the royal nursery's windows. That made the total distance 26 miles, 385 yards, the distance that all marathoners run today.

These Games also introduced the first clouds of political conflict that so often define today's Olympic experience. Ireland boycotted after its athletes were told they would have to compete under the British flag. And the United States became an enemy of the Empire after discus thrower Martin Sheridan refused to dip the American flag when passing King Edward during the opening ceremony. The Irish-American famously explained, "This flag dips to no earthly king."

An act of defiance that cost one of his countrymen a gold medal and led to one of the most notorious finishes in Olympic history.

Only four runners advanced to the finals of the 400 (meters, after the British reluctantly agreed to adopt the metric system for the Olympics): one Briton, Wyndham Halswelle, and three Americans, William Robbins, John Carpenter, and John Taylor.

The drama and controversy unfolded as the runners reached the final straightaway, with Robbins in the lead. Carpenter and Halswelle had been battling it out for second place, but as the runners began to make a push past the slowing Robbins, Carpenter got there first, preventing the hometown Halswelle from making his move.

Blocking another runner was permitted by the American athletics federation in 1908, but not by the British—who comprised 100% of the judges and officials working these Olympics. And as Carpenter approached the finishing tape to claim his victory, the track judge called "foul" and removed the tape before Carpenter could break it.

After an hour of deliberation, the officials (exclusively British, and still pretty ticked off that a bunch of Yankees would disrespect their King) determined that Carpenter would be disqualified and the race would be rerun the following day. Predictably the other two American runners, Robbins and Taylor, refused to run in protest.

That left the reluctant Halswelle as the only remaining runner, and it gives him the dubious distinction of being the only Olympic champion and gold medalist to ever win in a walkover.

Following the 1908 London Games, the International Olympic Committee (IOC) decided that from then on judges would be drawn from an international pool, rather than supplied by the host country—effectively ending any and all political interposition that would have otherwise haunted future Olympics. Right.

The IOC also determined that standardized rules needed to be drawn up for each sport. That led directly to the creation of the International Amateur Athletic Federation (IAAF), track and field's governing body, and its codification of rules for competition.

Cold War Compromised
Munich 1972: Men's Basketball Gold Medal Game

Never before, or since, had an Olympic Games exemplified the highs of the movement's ideals while also illustrating the tragic lows of the human experience as did the 1972 Munich Olympics.

These were the Games of Mark Spitz and his seven gold medals; the Games of seventeen-year-old Olga Korbut, the media darling who won three golds in gymnastics; and of course, the Games of the massacre of eleven Israeli athletes by the Arab terrorist group Black September.

They were also the Olympics of the most controversial basketball game ever played.

1972 Men's Basketball Gold Medal Game: The Soviet Union, after a pair of gifted second chances gives them the winning basket, celebrate their first ever win over the United States.

Since basketball first became an Olympic sport in 1936, the Americans had never lost, winning seven straight gold medals and fifty-five straight games. And with legendary coach Henry Iba, a winner of gold in 1964 and 1968, again at the helm, the United States went to Munich in 1972 as overwhelming favorites despite being the youngest team in U.S. basketball history and suffering the absence of perhaps the country's best amateur player, UCLA's Bill Walton.

The Americans, as expected, cruised into the gold-medal game, winning their eight games (taking their overall unbeaten streak to sixty-three) by an average score of 76-43. The Soviet Union, also the easy winners of eight in a row, joined the United States in the finals for the fifth time in six Olympics (1968 was the lone exception, after Yugoslavia stunned the Soviets 63-62 in the semifinals).

The championship game was more than just a battle between two basketball teams. This was the height of the Cold War. It was superpower vs. superpower, a contest of ideologies, and it was all done against the backdrop of the raging war in Vietnam.

From the moment the game tipped off, the favored Americans had their hands full. The Soviets were bigger, more experienced, and as it turned out, better than expected. And by the time the clock wound down to five minutes to play, the Soviet Union had extended its 5-point halftime lead all the way to 12.

But the United States mounted a frantic comeback. And with only 3 seconds on the clock, and now trailing by 1, American guard Doug Collins went to the free throw line with a chance to secure the gold medal. The future NBA head coach, and current collegian at Illinois State, sank both of his pressure shots to give the United States its first lead of the game, 50-49.

The Soviets quickly inbounded the ball, but missed a desperation final shot, giving the gold to the United States. But in the brief celebration chaos that followed, the referees emerged, claiming that the action had actually been stopped with 1 second left because the Soviet bench had called timeout.

The validity of that alleged timeout—when it was called (during or after Collins's free throws) and who called it—has forever been in question. But the referees that day decided to reset the clock and give the Soviets one more chance.

Again, the Soviets inbounded the basketball. And justly, before the Russians could capitalize on the extra opportunity, the horn sounded, and the Americans again stormed the court as Olympic champions. A second celebration that was short lived when R. William Jones, the long-time head of the International

Amateur Basketball Association, made the unprecedented decision to intervene.

The man largely responsible for bringing basketball to the international community, and the first non-American to be elected to the Basketball Hall of Fame, told the game officials that they had to put 3 seconds back on the clock and rerun the play because of a timing malfunction.

Later, when explaining his decision, Jones uttered the words that have haunted his legacy as a basketball pioneer: "The Americans have to learn how to lose, even when they think they are right."

The third time was the Soviet Union's charm and the USA's curse. Following a completed long pass down court, forward Aleksandr Belov split American defenders Jim Forbes and Kevin Joyce and made the most talked about layup in Olympic basketball history, giving gold to the Soviets.

The United States immediately filed a formal, and futile, protest. The politics of the day ruled everything, especially the Olympic Games. With three of the five judges who heard the protest hailing from Communist Bloc countries, the final vote, predictably, was 3-2 in favor of the Russians.

For the first time in Olympic basketball history, the United States would go home without the gold. And, as things turned out, they didn't go home with the silver medal either. The team, driven by the indignation of being cheated, voted unanimously to refuse their silvers and skip the medal ceremony in protest.

The feeling was so intense that team captain Kenny Davis actually put a provision in his will to prevent his family from ever accepting the medal.

To this day, all twelve unclaimed silver medals from 1972 remain locked in a Swiss vault.

Jobbed, Pound-for-Pound

Seoul 1988: Light-Middleweight Boxing Finals

What transpired in Seoul, South Korea, in 1988 might be more accurately referred to as the Soul-less Olympic Games. Student riots and security fears concerning the jilted communist North Koreans dominated the pre-Olympic news. But once the Games kicked off on September 17, those headlines were quickly replaced by the biggest doping and bribery scandals to ever hit the Olympics.

There was the embarrassment of Ben Johnson, for two days the world's fastest man, until he was stripped of the gold medal after failing a drug test. Carl Lewis and Linford Christie, the two sprinters who finished behind Johnson, and Olympic champions in '84 and '92 respectively, moved up to take gold and silver—although both would be dogged by drug allegations in later years.

American sprinter Florence Griffith-Joyner won three gold medals in Seoul. But she also had to endure days of reporter's questions about drugs, and innuendo that changes in her physique were caused by increased levels of testosterone. After Flo-Jo set a world record in the 200 meters, silver medalist Grace Jackson is said to have shouted to trackside reporters, "Jamaicans do it naturally!"

And then there is the case of Roy Jones Jr., with a twist. Instead of being the perpetrator of controversy, Jones was the unmitigated victim.

When Jones went to Seoul in 1988, he was already a shining young star in the boxing world, having won Golden Gloves championships in two weight classes the previous two years. And everyone assumed that the nineteen-year-old Floridian was a cinch to add even more gold to his trophy case at the Olympics.

What they failed to factor in, however, was just how determined the hometown Koreans were to win a gold of their own.

When the overmatched Si-Hun Park met Jones in the light-middleweight finals, Park was already embroiled in controversy, having won four straight controversial matches, including one by disabling an opponent with a low blow. And it was clear from the start that the South Korean had no business being in the same ring as Jones.

The best that can be said about Park's performance is that he survived. He was thoroughly dominated by the quicker American, getting outpunched over the three rounds by an incredible 86 to 32. But Park did not get knocked out, and in this case, that was enough.

Shockingly, Park was awarded the gold medal by a judge's vote of 3-2—a decision that was so stunning that, after it was announced, Park actually turned to Jones and apologized. Then in a perverse twisting of the knife, those same judges named Jones the Games' Most Outstanding Boxer.

How, you ask, could three supposed boxing experts so badly misjudge a gold medal bout? Simple, they were paid to.

An uncovered report in the archives of the Stasi, the former East German secret police, said that a Korean millionaire had bribed senior boxing federation officials to judge fights in favor of Korean boxers. Argentine judge Osbaldo Bisbal said that he was replaced on the judging panel moments before the gold-medal match because he wouldn't take a bribe. And Morocco's Hiouad Larbi, one of the judges responsible for giving the gold to Park, admitted to reporters that he had in fact taken money to fill out a false scorecard.

Yet in 1997, in all its infinite wisdom, the IOC determined through its own internal investigation that, despite the Stasi report, Larbi's admission, and the only commonsense explanation as to how three judges could simultaneously be so immeasurably wrong, no bribe had taken place and therefore Park's gold medal would stand.

Jones, who went on to have a stellar pro career and carry the unofficial title of "Best Pound-for-Pound Boxer" in the world, said, "The Olympics as a child really inspired me. It gave me something to reach for, it gave me a dream. And then the Olympics shattered my dream."

Poached Hamm
Athens 2004: Men's Gymnastics All-Around Finals

In 2004 the Summer Olympics returned to its ancient origins in Athens. But it was the modern Olympic rivalry between the United States and South Korea, born from bribery in 1988, that would dominate the headlines at the Games' most glamorous event, gymnastics.

Korean sports fans have long memories—even if they're a little fuzzy on the details. At the Salt Lake City Winter Games in 2002 when short-track speed skater Kim Dong-sung was disqualified in the 1,500-meter finals, giving the gold to American Apolo Anton Ohno, the Koreans reacted with righteous indignation, treating the incident as an international affront of the highest order—conveniently forgetting the hair-splitting details of Roy Jones Jr. and the criminal acts of Korea's boxing federation in 1988.

Ohno's "theft" trumped all, and the feelings of resentment ran deep. Four months later during the World Cup soccer match between Korea and the United States, Ahn Jung-hwan celebrated his second-half game-tying goal by simulating a speedskater. Ahn then dedicated the goal to Kim, the victimized Winter Olympian, and all of his grudge-carrying countrymen.

Which takes us to 2004 and the men's gymnastics all-around finals.

When American Paul Hamm stumbled into the judge's table after failing to stick the landing on his vault, the twenty-one-year-old twin brother of fellow gymnast Morgan Hamm thought that his twelfth-place hole would prove to be too big. His dream of becoming the first American all-around men's champion was over. He would need a pair of 9.8s in his final two events just to get within sniffing distance of the medal stand.

But incredibly, Hamm scored a 9.837 on the parallel bars, moving him into fourth place and keeping the dream alive. Then, needing the performance of his life on the high bar, his best event, Hamm came up with a second-straight 9.837. Not only was Hamm on the medal stand, he was on top of it—pulling off what U.S. teammate Brett McClure called "the greatest comeback in gymnastics history."

The joy of that historic moment, however, was very short lived.

Romanian Ioan Suciu, the eventual fourth-place finisher, said, "The USA got more than it deserved." Silver medalist, and South Korean, Kim Dae-eun said he was angered by the result.

Those complaints were nothing more than sour grapes. By all impartial observers, Hamm's performances did warrant the scores he was given, putting the defending world champion ahead of Suciu and Kim because of his merits as a clutch-performing gymnast. The same dismissal, though, cannot be given to South Korean bronze medalist Yang Tae-young.

When Yang performed his parallel-bar routine prior to Hamm's comeback, the judges unfairly lowered his starting value by 0.1 points. Had his routine started with the correct 10.0 value, instead of the 9.9 he was given, Yang would have leapfrogged over Kim and Hamm to win the gold medal by 0.51 points.

Two days later Fédération Internationale de Gymnastique (FIG) president Bruno Grandi admitted the mistake by upholding the Korean protest and suspending three judges. But he also said that Hamm would keep his gold medal. Then, six days after that, Grandi took the coward's route by publicly declaring Yang the "true winner" and saying that it was up to Hamm to correct the mistake himself by giving the gold medal to Yang "as the ultimate demonstration of fair play."

So with the gutless Grandi on his side, and the backing of the Korean Olympic Committee, Yang took his case to wrest the gold from Hamm all the way to the Court of Arbitration for Sport. It should be noted that before the Korean took that step, which the Americans vigorously fought, U.S. Olympic officials said they would support a bid to award Yang a duplicate gold medal.

Finally, on October 21, more than two months after the competition in Athens was completed, the CAS handed down its ruling: "An error identified with the benefit of hindsight, whether admitted or not, cannot be a ground for reversing a result of a competition."

The gold was finally Hamm's, officially. And Yang respected the ruling, opting instead to look to the future.

Showing the Olympic spirit that was lacking in so many of the other players at the center of this storm, the Korean declared, "I will have a gold medal hung around my neck at the next Olympics in Beijing, without fail."

And if there is justice in the world, he will.

French-Fried Figure Skating
Salt Lake City 2002: Pairs Figure Skating Finals

French writer Jules Renard wrote:

> *La vérité vaut bien qu'on passé quelques années sans la trouver.*
> "Truth is more valuable if it takes you a few years to find it."

In the case of the French figure-skating judges at the 2002 Winter Olympics, it took just a few days.

Under the cloud of conspiracy that saw a number of IOC

2002 Pairs Figure Skating: Duplicate gold medals are awarded to Canadians Jamie Salé and David Pelletier after a judge's scandal is uncovered.

members resign for inappropriately accepting high-value gifts in exchange for their vote to award the Games to Salt Lake City, and in the shadows of unprecedented security following the 9/11 attacks five months earlier, 2,399 athletes from seventy-seven nations descended upon Utah's Wasatch Mountains.

But sixteen days of competition later and after seventy-eight events had been completed, the fame of two athletes, Jamie Salé and David Pelletier, ascended above the rest and carried beyond the Games.

Judging Olympic figure skating is purely subjective. And by subjective we mean subject to deals, favors, and bribes. And during the pairs figure skating finals in Salt Lake City, this reality shook the sport to its core and made household names of the pair of Canadians. (The Russian team involved in the scandal would have also probably become household names, if anyone could in fact pronounce them.)

During their long program to decide the gold medal, Salé and Pelletier skated flawlessly, raising the expectation of everyone in the crowd that they had just witnessed the gold-medal performance. But when the judges' scores came in, the Canadians had to settle for silver. The Russian pair of Yelena Berezhnaya and Anton Sikharulidze, even though they had stumbled out of a jump and the Canadians had made no such mistake, secured the pair's gold for Russia for the eleventh consecutive time.

The vote was close at 5-4, with judges from Russia, Poland, Ukraine, China, and France favoring the Russian pair. But anyone who saw both pairs skate knew that something fishy was afoot, beyond the typical block voting that had become the norm in skating and almost always broke along old Cold War lines.

The International Skating Union almost immediately launched an "internal assessment" to ensure, as they put it, "ISU rules and procedures have been respected."

The focus of the investigation was French judge Marie-Reine Le Gougne, the so-called gold-medal swing vote. And when investigators questioned her about the reasons she cast the deciding vote for the Russians, she confessed that she had been pressured by French figure skating federation president Didier Gailhaguet to favor the Russians in pairs, in exchange for their support for the French skaters in the ice dancing finals.

Gailhaguet denied the charge, and Le Gougne would later recant, saying that she'd only pointed the finger at Gailhaguet out of fear. But the rather large and embarrassing cat was out of the bag. With Le Gougne's original admissions circulating in the world press, the need for swift action became paramount.

Four days after the two sets of skaters had been thrown into the cauldron of controversy, the IOC awarded Salé and Pelletier a duplicate set of gold medals. Following the ceremony, in which both couples received standing ovations, the exhausted and at times unfairly criticized Sikharulidze said, "I am so happy, because I think now it is finished."

Finished, but in the end, fortuitous.

All four skaters emerged from the Salt Lake mess with grace and dignity still firmly attached, as well as a newly cultivated renown that opened doors for them to skate and tour professionally. The two twosomes off the ice also became the best of friends.

Le Gougne, who along with French federation president Gailhaguet, was suspended for the 2006 Torino Olympics, said that in the aftermath of Salt Lake City she had "terrible suffering" and "contemplated suicide."

But before you start to feel sorry for her, she also now arrogantly takes credit for the new scoring system that was implemented directly because of the scandal she created.

In an interview shortly before the 2006 Olympics, Le Gougne said, "World skating has paid me homage. When the judges come to see me they said: 'Marie-Reine, the new scoring system is so great. Thank you, Marie-Reine, because without you there would not have been a new scoring system.'"

Arrogance on a par with executives from Enron, WorldCom, and Tyco taking credit for corporate reform in America.

Pool Payback
Athens 2004: Men's 200-meter Backstroke

In the world of competitive swimming, there are few things more precious than an Olympic gold medal. It is how the all-time greats of the sport, like Mark Spitz, Tracy Caulkins, Matt Biondi, Janet Evans, and Michael Gross, will forever be defined.

But sometimes, as happened at the Olympic Aquatic Center in Athens in 2004, that pinnacle of performance can be sullied by the petty revenge of an insulted judge.

At the Sydney Games in 2000, seventeen-year-old American Aaron Peirsol missed Olympic gold in the 200-meter backstroke by less than a second, losing to teammate and friend Lenny Krayzelburg. But by 2002, when he was still just a teenager, Peirsol had shattered all of his mentor's world records and established himself as the backstroke king, the best in the world and the favorite to take double gold in Athens.

In the pool, Peirsol's 2004 Olympics began as expected. He won the 100-meter backstroke gold medal. But unexpectedly, and much to the chagrin of his coaches, the day before his first win Peirsol had started a controversial verbal war with his judges.

Amid accusations that he used an illegal dolphin kick, Japanese swimmer Kosuke Kitajima won the 100-meter breaststroke by a slim margin over American Brendan Hansen. But while Hansen stayed above the controversy, refusing to blame the judges, Peirsol wasn't so diplomatic, telling reporters, "The whole stadium saw what happened. It's Brendan's gold medal. It breaks your heart. It's cheating."

Peirsol had called the judge's competence and integrity into question. A no-no for a swimmer who still had events to swim. And when the television replays backed up Peirsol's claims, the judges who'd let Kitajima's gold medal stand faced added embarrassment, adding to the baggage that at least one judge carried into the 200-meter backstroke finals.

As he had done in every 200-meter backstroke since the 2000 Olympics, Peirsol won. In fact, he won this race by a comfy 2.4 seconds. But when Peirsol glanced up at the scoreboard to celebrate his second gold medal, he noticed the dreaded "DSQ" next to his name. French judge Denis Cadon, in a ruling that left everyone at the pool in stunned confusion, claimed that the American made an illegal turn at the 150-meter mark.

But before the American team could formally file its protest, as it planned to do, Peirsol's gold medal swim was restored twenty intense minutes later, a turn of events that raised some serious questions about the judges involved.

Austrian Markus Rogan, the swimmer who would have been elevated from silver to gold if Peirsol's disqualification had stood, told reporters he thought the judge's decision was fallout from Peirsol's previous comments.

Rogan said, "I believe politics are everywhere. I believe there might have been something about Aaron being very outspoken about his friend Brendan. I don't want to pass judgment on the referees but . . . people should do their jobs properly."

Rogan went on to describe his feelings about losing, then winning, then losing again, telling reporters, "After the race I asked Aaron, 'What the hell happened?' and he said he had swum a fair race. I knew right there that he swam a fair race because Aaron Peirsol doesn't lie. I feel like I am the second-best backstroker in the world, and at the end of the day, nothing's changed."

But what did change, within twenty minutes, was the claim by French judge Cadon that Peirsol had violated the rules enough to lose a gold medal, a claim that is life-changing for the swimmer involved, and shouldn't be taken lightly.

So why was such an important ruling overturned so quickly?

The official reason given by the Fédération Internationale de Natation (FINA) was a technical one. The alleged violation by Peirsol wasn't adequately explained in "the working language of FINA," either English or French. So on a technicality, similar to evidence being thrown out in a court of law, the disqualification couldn't stand.

But a few days later it was revealed that the judge's report given to the referee, which was not in "the working language of FINA," was in fact left blank. Nothing, in any language, was written. And according to FINA executive director Cornel Marculescu, that is "really strange."

Strange enough to have everyone in the sport quietly

wondering if this had been an orchestrated attempt to get back at the outspoken Peirsol by tarnishing one of his golds.

And in the world where athletics meets international politics, stranger things have happened.

Curtains for Quance

U.S. Olympic Swimming Trials 1996:
Women's 400-meter Individual Medley

The American way of choosing its Olympic team, the Olympic trials, is the paragon of fair play. It epitomizes a level playing field. No matter where an athlete ranks, what medals or awards they've won in the past, or what companies have signed them to million-dollar endorsement deals, everyone has an equal chance to make the Olympic team. All you have to do is finish in the top two.

However, this egalitarian system of selection that in many ways is an ironic gradation of democracy from Ancient Olympia can also be cold, cruel, and unforgiving.

Just ask decathlete Dan O'Brien, who, because of a miscalculated pole vault at the U.S. Olympic trials, dropped from gold medal favorite in Barcelona—and darling of Reebok—to nothing more than a cheerleader for teammate Dave Johnson.

The history of heartbreaks is even longer in swimming. In 1972 Kurt Krumpholz set a world record in the 400-meter freestyle, but failed to make the Olympic team. In 1988 Pablo Morales was the American record holder in two events and a world-record holder in a third. But the winner of eleven individual NCAA championships at Stanford failed to make the Seoul Olympics.

And then there is the tough-luck tale of Kristine Quance.

Weakened from a bout with mononucleosis, the then-seventeen-year-old failed to qualify for the Olympic team in 1992. Four years later and four years better, and with the Olympic

Games to be held on home soil, Quance was the favorite to win gold in the 400-meter individual medley in Atlanta. But again, the fickle finger of fate intervened.

In the preliminaries of the U.S. trials, it was clear that the summer of '96 was her time to shine. Quance raced out to a big early lead, keeping that pace the entire 400 meters for a world record time of 4:42.28, a full four seconds faster than her nearest competitor.

But instead of experiencing the celebration of her world-record-setting swim while preparing for a comfortable final heat later that afternoon, Quance was victimized by the inverse of emotions. She'd been disqualified for an illegal turn, instantly ending her Olympic dream.

The rule reads:

> *Once the wall is touched, the swimmer may turn in any manner but the shoulders must be at or past the vertical toward the breast when the swimmer leaves the wall. The swimmer must have attained breaststroke form before the first arm stroke.*

According to Quance's coach at USC, Mark Schubert, and nearly every other swimming expert on hand that day, it's a call that's never made. Certainly, it's never called at the world-championship level when an Olympic-team bid is on the line and the swimmer so clearly dominates the field that even if she did gain a slight advantage by executing a borderline turn, the edge is immaterial.

Immaterial. But not inconsequential.

Unlike the prevailing cooler heads that eventually overturned the call against Aaron Peirsol in Athens, reinstating his gold-medal swim, no such absolution was given to Kristine Quance. She went on to finish her collegiate career with eight individual NCAA championships, and would later become a successful swim coach in Southern California. But because one set of eyes out of a thousand saw a turn violation in the churning waters of the Indiana University Natatorium in 1996, Quance never got her individual Olympic gold medal.

Boxing's Un-Holy Burglary
Los Angeles 1984: Light Heavyweight Boxing Semifinals

Sports fans know all about the great quarterback class of 1983. It produced three Pro Football Hall of Famers: John Elway, Dan Marino, and Jim Kelly. Over the sixteen years that followed the draft (1983–1998), eleven Super Bowls featured an '83 alum. The group combined to throw 1,175 touchdown passes. And twenty-four times a member of the class was selected to the Pro Bowl. An even more impressive feat when you consider that the six first-round quarterbacks were all drafted by AFC teams, and competing for the same roster spots.

The quantity and quality of its talent—and we're not even including fellow 83ers Eric Dickerson and Darrell Green—has never had an equal. And it's unlikely that it ever will. But there was one group of athletes, just one year later, which has to be considered a close second.

The 1984 United States Olympic boxing team ruled Los Angeles. Of the twelve boxing gold medals given out, nine of them went to Americans. And of those nine Olympic champions, Meldrick Taylor, Pernell Whitaker, Mark Breland, and Frank Tate all went on to capture world championships.

And just imagine how impressive this list would be if we could include Evander Holyfield, one of the true all-time greats, but just a bronze medalist in 1984 because of Yugoslavian referee Gligorije Novicic's very questionable decision.

Fighting in the semifinals against Kevin Barry of New Zealand, the reigning American Golden Gloves champion was cruising to victory—until a harmless clinch knocked out his gold-medal hopes. As the two fighters held each other, Holyfield cocked his powerful left arm back to throw a punch, when at the same exact moment the referee yelled "break."

Asking a quick and aggressive fighter blessed with the abilities of Holyfield to pull his punch in mid-throw is a lot like asking that fighter to take up ballroom dancing on national television. It's the kind of quixotic fool's illusion that's plagued the denizens of amateur boxing rings and narcissistic network boardrooms since the dawn of time.

Barry broke, but Holyfield still punched, and a split-second later Barry went down. The referee counted the New Zealander out, even though he was back on his feet by three, and then turned to the favored American and discriminately disqualified him.

That controversial decision by Novicic effectively handed the gold medal to fellow countryman Anton Josipovic. Because of the concussion suffered from Holyfield's punch, Barry wasn't able to compete in the gold-medal match, and Josipovic was declared the winner.

Josipovic, for his part, understood his good, and perhaps improper, fortune. During the medal ceremony, in a display of Olympic sportsmanship, the gold medalist grabbed the bronze medal-settling Holyfield, pulled him to the top of the medal stand, and raised the arm of the future four-time world heavyweight champion.

Six years later, shortly after beating Buster Douglas to become the undisputed heavyweight title holder, Holyfield began to mentor and encourage a young amateur boxer named David Tua. Holyfield took the nineteen-year-old under his wing at the request of Tua's manager, Kevin Barry.

Olympic Inequality
Los Angeles 1932/London 1948: Women's Track and Field

At the 2004 Summer Olympics in Athens, 44% of the athletes were women. The Games in Athens were also the first to be hosted by a woman mayor, Dora Bakoyianni, and led by a woman organizer, Gianna Angelopoulos-Daskalaki.

But the very facts that make the Olympics' twenty-first-century return to Greece worth noting as a triumph of equality also serve as a reminder of the hard and unjust road of inequities that many female Olympians had to travel.

Ancient Greece, despite its passel of forward-thinking philosophers, was as backward and sexist as any place in world history. Women Olympians were strictly forbidden. And if a married woman was caught entering the games as a spectator, the punishment was death. Virgins and prostitutes, however, were allowed, and sometimes presented as awards to the athletes.

When Pierre de Coubertin revived the modern games in 1896, it was decided that executing female spectators would probably be bad for business, but on-the-field participation would remain an all-male affair. The baron felt that instead of seeking glory for herself, a woman's more rewarding role would be as her son's encourager.

That stance would soften, and eventually women began to trickle into the Games as athletes in the early years of the twentieth century. But decades would pass before the exclusively male International Olympic Committee (the first woman member was elected in 1981) would relax its rules on participation, rules that prevented scores of athletes from winning medals, and at least two women from making history.

Babe Didrikson went into the 1932 Los Angeles Olympics as the world's best female athlete. And not just best of her time; the best of all time. Prior to becoming a track-and-field star, and qualifying for five events at the Los Angeles Olympics, Didrikson was the country's best basketball player. She also played tennis and volleyball, and got the nickname Babe because of her prowess with a baseball bat.

Picture a female Michael Jordan/Tiger Woods/Carl Lewis hybrid, and you've got Babe Didrikson.

Heading into the '32 Games, the twenty-one-year-old Didrikson should have been the favorite to win gold medals in all five events she'd qualified in. Of course, that would have required that she enter all five events, which she couldn't. The rules prevented women from entering more than three individual events. At the time women were also banned from runs longer than 200 meters because they were deemed too dangerous for the fairer sex.

The IOC's pigheadedness forced the "fair" Didrikson to skip the discus and long jump, two of her best events. But she did win gold in the javelin and 80-meter hurdles, setting world records in both. Unfortunately she had to settle for silver in the high jump when her jumping style was declared illegal. Didrikson was leading with her head and not her body, much like the "Fosbury Flop" made famous by Dick Fosbury in 1968, which is now not only legal, it's the standard.

Following the Olympics, and looking for a new challenge, Didrikson decided to take up golf. And before cancer would tragically take her two decades later at the age of 45, she won ten major golf championships, helped found the LPGA, and six times was named Associated Press Female Athlete of the Year.

Sixteen years after Didrikson's shortened Olympics, the best woman athlete on the planet was the Netherlands' Fanny Blankers-Koen. But at thirty years old, having lost her prime Olympic years to the war-cancelled games of 1940 and 1944, Blankers-Koen was considered too old. And after she engaged in the presumed athletic career-ending event of childbirth—twice—most of the press covering the 1948 London Olympics had written her off.

But that was a mistake. This mother of two was also the holder of six world records, and now a little angered by her dismissal, she went to London determined to prove everyone wrong. And she did just that, capturing Olympic gold in the 100 meters, 200 meters, 80-meter hurdles, and the 4x100-meter relay, becoming the first ever mom/Olympic champion in history.

Her Olympic games would have been even more historic if she hadn't been forced to skip both the long jump and high jump, because again, she'd already competed in the IOC's maximum allowable number of individual events for a woman.

And Blankers-Koen, named the IAAF's Female Athlete of the Century in 1999 (very much to her humble surprise), was a safe bet to do well in the pair of jumping events. She was, after all, the world record holder in both, two of the twelve world records that she would set during her attitude-altering career.

As it stands today, Blankers-Koen's four track and field gold medals in one Olympics tied the record set by Jesse Owens and later equaled by Carl Lewis. But if the woman nicknamed "the Flying Housewife" had been allowed to compete in her full compliment of skills, she no doubt would have eclipsed even those two all-time legends.

The opening of the Olympic Creed, as chosen by de Coubertin in 1908, reads: *The most important thing in the Olympic Games is not to win, but to take part.*

But at one time, if you were a woman chasing the Olympic dream, "to take part" came with conditions.

The Greatest Athlete in the World
Stockholm 1912: Decathlon and Pentathlon

Jim Thorpe is arguably the greatest athlete the world has ever known. There was almost nothing that involved sport where Thorpe didn't excel. He was a major league baseball player, the

1912 Decathlon and Pentathlon: Native American Jim Thorpe dominated the Olympic Games in Stockholm.

first true superstar in professional football, and the most well-rounded track and field athlete ever.

But like so many of the world's great masters, his life's highest achievements were bounded by tragedy, controversy, and injustice.

Born into the poverty of Indian Territory (what is now Oklahoma), Thorpe was given the Native American name Wa-Tho-Huk, which prophetically means *Bright Path*. But initially for Thorpe, his bright path to greatness was a journey fraught with pain. His twin brother, Charlie, died of pneumonia at age eight. And by the time he was a teenager attending Carlisle Indian School in Pennsylvania, both his parents had died.

But it was at Carlisle that Thorpe would meet the man who gave him direction, focus, and ultimate fame. That man was Glenn Scobey "Pop" Warner, one of the most influential college football coaches in history.

Already a member of Carlisle's lacrosse and baseball teams, Thorpe became a track and field star under Warner's tutelage. And as the leader of Warner's football team, Thorpe skyrocketed from schoolyard promise to national prominence. The All-American running back/defensive back/kicker/punter scored every point in Carlisle's 18-15 upset victory over Harvard.

The following summer Thorpe made the U.S. Olympic team, putting his incredible athletic gifts on display at the 1912 Stockholm Olympics.

Thorpe won four of the five events of the pentathlon, easily taking the gold medal. And in the decathlon Thorpe placed in the top four in all ten events, winning the gold with a world-record-shattering 8,412 points.

Legend has it that as Sweden's King Gustav V presented Thorpe with his medals, he said, "You, sir, are the greatest athlete in the world." To which Thorpe replied, "Thanks, King."

Following his return, which began with a ticker-tape parade down New York's Broadway, the conquering hero spent another fall dominating the gridiron. Thorpe, in his second consecutive All-American season, led Carlisle to the 1912 national championship, highlighted by a 27-6 demolition of Army. That afternoon a young West Point cadet named Dwight D. Eisenhower was injured while trying to tackle Thorpe.

In early 1913, on top of the world and preparing to begin a major league baseball career with the New York Giants, the roof suddenly caved in on Thorpe's status as an American hero. Writer Roy Johnson wrote a story for the *Worcester (Mass.) Telegraph* that alleged Thorpe's play-for-pay past in baseball's Class D Eastern Carolina League.

Thorpe confirmed the story, but asked that the Amateur Athletic Union (AAU) forgive his transgression as nothing more than a mistake made by a naïve schoolboy who needed the $15 a week to eat in the summers of 1909 and 1910. But that plea fell on deaf ears, and cruelly, Thorpe's gold medals from 1912 were no longer his.

Thorpe would go on to play major league baseball for six years, lead the Canton Bulldogs to football championships in 1916, 1917, and 1919, and become the first president of the American Professional Football Association (the precursor to the NFL) in 1920. But the fouling of his self-described "proudest moment," winning his two gold medals in Stockholm, continued to haunt Thorpe.

For years, efforts were made to restore Thorpe's Olympic medals. The rules of 1912 stated that officials had only thirty days to question an athlete's amateur status, and Thorpe's $15 offense wasn't known until six months after the Games concluded. But for years those appeals and protests failed.

Avery Brundage, a teammate of Thorpe's on the 1912 U.S. decathlon team, became the president of the AAU in 1928, the U.S. Olympic Committee (USOC) in 1929, and the IOC in 1945. And until his retirement in 1972, he was the man most responsible for the continued injustice.

Brundage was a strong supporter of the Olympics' amateur-only policy. But he was also a fan of Adolf Hitler's Nazi Germany, responsible for suspending Tommie Smith and John Carlos for their medal-stand display of Black Power in 1968, and strongly opposed to excluding countries from the Olympics because of their apartheid policies.

There is no evidence that Brundage kept ruling against Thorpe for fifty years because Thorpe was an American Indian who had upstaged him during his own Olympic appearance. But in matters of race, Brundage's hard-line stance is well documented.

Finally, in 1982, seventy years after Thorpe captured the world's imagination in Stockholm and almost thirty years after he died penniless in California, tarnished by his place in Olympic infamy, commonsense justice prevailed—almost.

The IOC did vote to reinstate Thorpe's two gold medals. But since the two silver medalists were elevated to gold in 1913 when Thorpe was stripped of his two victories, the "greatest athlete in the world" could only be considered an Olympic cochampion.

The Longest Ski Jump
Chamonix 1924: Ski Jump

Russian mathematician Tobias Dantzig said, "Mathematics is the supreme judge; from its decisions there is no appeal."

Fortunately for ski jumper Anders Haugen, Dantzig wasn't completely right. When the sums involved result in a mysterious miscalculation, judgments can be vacated as long as you're willing to suspend expectations for a snappy solution.

The first Winter Olympics in 1924 was a long time in the making, and a near international incident in the actualization.

The origin of the Winter Games actually dates back to 1870 when, following the Franco-Prussian war, the French began to promote skiing among its youth, hoping that they could eventually build a regiment of ski troops comparable to Norway's. That led to state backing for French ski clubs, and government dollars to help build winter-sports facilities in a number of mountain towns. And when the International Olympic Committee was founded in 1895, Pierre de Coubertin—good Frenchman that he was—signed a Winter Olympic Games into its charter.

The implementation, however, was still decades away.

Most of the nations involved in the early Olympic movement had no interest in Winter Games. And of the nations that did, most of those didn't have the facilities to host them. And those nations that met both criteria of ambition and ability—specifically the Scandinavian countries of Norway, Sweden, and Finland—had their own ideas, different from the IOC, on how international competitions should be contested.

Following an aborted attempt to host the Winter Games in Berlin in 1916 (World War I intervened), the first Winter Olympics were finally scheduled for Chamonix, France, in 1924. In order to get the Norwegians to show up and feel less threatened about the future of their own Nordic Games, the IOC declared that the Chamonix Games were not officially "Olympic," a designation that was in name only (athletes still took the Olympic oath), and one that was officially changed by the IOC a year later.

Ironically, but not unexpectedly, it was the reluctant Norwegian team that dominated the medal stand. They won an Olympic-high four of sixteen events, and finished the Games with seventeen total medals. Leading the way for Norway was Thorleif Haug, a winner of two golds in cross-country skiing, the gold in Nordic combined, and a bronze medal in ski jumping.

To commemorate that first Winter Olympic team, Norway planned to honor their heroes on the fiftieth anniversary of their triumph in Chamonix. And of course, even though he had long since passed away, that meant honoring the Winter Games' first star, Thorleif Haug.

But a funny thing happened on the way to that celebration. Norwegian sports historian Jakov Vaage uncovered a scoring discrepancy in the ski-jumping competition.

The official result had Haug taking the bronze with 18.000 points, just ahead of American Anders Haugen, a Norwegian immigrant who'd scored 17.916 points. But when Vaage did his own independent calculations, using ski jumping's mathematical formula that adds or subtracts points based on each jump's relation to the "K Line" (analogous to par), Vaage discovered that Haug's overall tally had been inflated. Haug's proper score was 17.821, which would have dropped him to fourth place, elevating the four-time United States ski-jumping champion Haugen to bronze.

Vaage immediately informed the IOC of the fifty-year-old mistake. And with the backing of the exceedingly gracious daughter of Haug, a special ceremony was held in Oslo to award the bronze medal to its rightful owner.

On September 17, 1974, more than fifty years after he'd competed on the slopes of France, the eighty-six-year-old Anders Haugen, then a retired bricklayer from Minnesota, became the oldest medalist in Olympic history.

Decidedly Out of Sync
Barcelona 1992: Synchronized Swimming

The history of the Olympics is full of inspiring stories about athletes overcoming adversity.

There is the story of Karoly Takacs, a member of Hungary's pistol shooting team who lost his hand to an exploding grenade. Following the accident he secretly taught himself how to shoot left-handed, and then won gold medals in 1948 and 1952.

In 2000 Marla Runyon, legally blind since she was a child, made the U.S. Olympic track team and finished 8th in the 1500 meters at Sydney. Two years later she was the fastest American woman at the New York marathon.

And then there is the story of Canadian synchronized swimmer Sylvie Fréchette, who not only had to deal with tragedy in her personal life just days before the 1992 Olympics, she also had to overcome indiscriminate injustice in the pools of Barcelona.

Fréchette spent the first half of the summer of '92 with the burden of being the gold-medal favorite. She was the best synchronized swimmer in the world. But on July 18, just a week before the Olympic flame was to be lit, she returned home from practice to find her fiancé dead by his own hand.

With her high expectations now turned to excruciating pain, Fréchette mustered the quiet courage to board her plane to Barcelona four days later. And a week after that she was ready—as much as she could be under the circumstances—to fulfill her Olympic dream.

Going into the compulsory figures portion of the competition, Fréchette knew she needed to put some initial distance between herself and American rival Kristen Babb-Sprague. The compulsories were Fréchette's strength, and the place where she could make up for Babb-Sprague's superior free routine, which would be performed during day two of the competition.

But the one thing Fréchette couldn't account for was a judge's typo.

After Fréchette completed the final of four movements, fittingly called the "albatross," Brazilian judge Ana Maria da Silviera inadvertently punched in the score of 8.7. Flustered, because she'd meant to award the move with a 9.7, da Silviera tried to correct the mistake, but again pressed 8.7.

She then tried to communicate her error to the referee in charge, but her English was bad, he was Japanese, and by the time she had sufficiently explained herself, the computer had posted the score as official. At that point, nothing could be done.

The following day, after a Canadian protest was denied, da Silviera's mistake provided the margin of victory. Babb-Sprague won the gold while Fréchette, who called the affair an extension of her "nightmare," settled for silver.

Led by IOC executive board member Dick Pound, himself a former Canadian Olympic swimmer, months of protests followed. And finally, in December of 1993, justice prevailed. In front of 2,000 fans in Montreal, Fréchette was able to trade in her silver for the duplicate gold medal that she deserved. Duplicate, because Babb-Sprague was allowed to keep hers.

Following her tragic and ultimately triumphant summer of '92, Fréchette went on to win a team silver medal in 1996. She then turned her abilities, fame, and years of public goodwill into a nine-year role as a performer and choreographer for Cirque du Soleil's Las Vegas water show, "O."

And all because of a typo.

Touch First, Finish Second
Rome 1960: Men's 100-meter Freestyle

The great sports rivalries of all time—Yankees-Red Sox, Michigan-Ohio State, Leafs-Canadiens—have all experienced an acceleration of animosity because of disputed defeats. Small slights become gaping wounds. Controversies charge battle cries. And flawed and false victories further fan the fray.

But when those moments of contention happen on that sport's biggest stage, the incident rises from heated occasion to historic milestone.

The American-Australian swimming rivalry, by far the longest running and most tightly contested Olympic-level rivalry in the world, can trace its roots back to the 1924 Olympics when Johnny Weissmuller led the United States to victory in the 800-meter freestyle relay. By the 1956 Games in Melbourne, the rivalry was a full-fledged fight, with the Aussies besting the United States by capturing fifteen medals, eight of which were gold, to the Americans' total of twelve with three gold medals.

But this rivalry, which would later spawn a special winner-take-all dual swim meet called "Duel in the Pool," hit its zenith in Rome in 1960.

The two men who were supposed to compete for gold, in what turned out to be the most talked-about 100-meter freestyle in Olympic history, were absent. The United States' top contender, Jeff Farrell, came down with appendicitis six days before the U.S. Olympic trials. With his heavily-taped, surgically repaired abdomen, Farrell finished fourth and failed to qualify. Then, out of fairness to the swimmers who had legitimately qualified, he turned down an offer to swim a special time trial after he'd recovered.

Australia's number one freestyler, and defending Olympic champion, was Jon Hendricks, who made the trip to Rome that summer as the odds-on favorite to take the gold again. But his dream to repeat met its demise with some bad Italian food. With what was euphemistically referred to as "Roman Tummy," Hendricks became very sick, dropped nearly twenty pounds, and lost in the semifinals.

So that left Aussie John Devitt, the new favorite, versus American Lance Larson, a twenty-year-old pre-dental student at Southern Cal whose best event was the 100-meter butterfly, which was not yet included in the Olympic program.

The two swimmers made the most of their opportunity, swimming an incredible and memorable race. But near the finish it looked like the gold was going to be Devitt's, until a furious close by Larson had the two of them touching the wall in a virtual dead heat. Most observers poolside had Larson winning by the thinnest of margins.

Devitt was among those who thought the American had won. The Australian gave Larson conciliatory congratulations before leaving the pool. All six of the timekeepers had Larson winning. The three clocks on Larson recorded his time as 55.0, 55.1, and 55.1 seconds, while the three timers for Devitt all clocked his time at 55.2. And the manually operated judging machine, which recorded the touch on three paper tapes, also made Larson the clear winner.

So where, you ask, was the controversy?

The timekeepers, on hand to record official times and world and Olympic records, were not used to decide the winning swimmer. And neither was the judging machine, which was being tested for the first time in 1960 and was still unofficial. The ultimate decision on a winner rested with a panel of very

1960 Men's 100-meter Freestyle: Controversial winner John Devitt stands with silver medalist Lance Larson on the medal stand in Rome.

human judges—which of course brings into play the very real possibility, and probability, of human error.

Of the three judges charged with deciding the gold medalist, two chose Devitt. But of the three judges assigned to choose the silver medalist, again, two chose Devitt, essentially making it a three-three split.

To resolve the impasse the judges then turned to the backup electronic timer, as they were supposed to do. And that timer had Larson (55.10) edging out Devitt (55.16) by what amounted to a four-inch difference.

So again, where was the controversy? Larson was the winner.

Chief judge Hans Runströmer, who clearly misunderstood his job description to mean something more along the lines of omnipotent ruler, decided, even though chief judges have never had the power to resolve disputed finishes, to break the judges' tie and give the gold to Devitt.

The Americans immediately questioned Runströmer's decision, in which he claimed to have clearly seen Devitt outtouch Larson. The claim proved false when *Sports Illustrated* published a photo that showed the chief judge opposite lane 8, five and six lanes away from the two swimmers, and at an angle where he couldn't possibly see the touch pads.

But even though Runströmer's decision was now valueless, the American appeals continued to be denied, appeals and protests that lasted four years, involved every member nation of FINA and the IOC, and were spearheaded by Max Ritter, the treasurer of the U.S. Olympic Committee who had made it his personal pursuit to see justice done for Larson.

In the end, it was action all for naught. The official results stood. Larson and Devitt were co-holders of the Olympic record of 55.2 seconds, but Devitt got the gold.

Sports officials must be able to bring control to chaos; understand fairness; promote safety and encourage good sportsmanship. A sports official must have the positive characteristics of a police officer, lawyer, judge, accountant, reporter, athlete and diplomat.

—THE NATIONAL ASSOCIATION OF SPORTS
OFFICIALS (*How to Become an Official*)

Many fans look upon the umpire as sort of a necessary evil to the luxury of baseball, like the odor that follows an automobile.

—CHRISTY MATHEWSON
HALL OF FAME PITCHER (1900–1916)

Imagine the job description: you're to run around in the mud on a Saturday afternoon and accept the malicious abuse of up to 40,000 people for ninety minutes plus injury time. Pay negligible.

—NICHOLAS ROYLE
ENGLISH NOVELIST, MANCHESTER BORN

POTPOURRI
(WITH DEFERENCE
TO ALEX TREBEK)

When a sport features a leisure activity that is sport in name only; or is regularly accompanied by a 12-pack of beer; or is only played in Canada; or when one of its players so much as gets breathed on, he writhes on the ground as if shot by an elephant gun (you know who you are, soccer players); or is known as much for its corruption as it is for competition (that's you, Don King), we place it in our miscellaneous anthology known as "potpourri."

In other words, if your sport's training table includes hot wings, has a uniform that utilizes plaid pants, has a vernacular that includes phrases like "turkey walk," "off the broom," and "backdoor burglar," requires you to bow to the Queen, is dominated by men with two first names and no front teeth, or has traditionally been controlled by guys named Lucky, Dutch, and Bugs, you'll find them here.

Not that we don't respect the sports that fall outside the category of the North American Big Four—baseball, football, basketball, and hockey—it's just that there are simply too many of them to warrant their own sections. There are nineteen sports alone that fall into the "racquet sports" category, and another thirty-one so-called "target sports," including marbles, mat ball, and the popular European pub sport of skittles, which itself has at last count seven different versions.

And that's to say nothing of the thirty-two "combat sports" that include wrestling, the many varieties and nationalities of the martial arts, and the hybrid sport of chess boxing. That's right, chess boxing, which alternates the action between four-minute rounds of chess and two-minute rounds in the ring. You win by knockout, checkmate, or a judge's decision.

And where there are judges, bad calls are soon to follow.

SOCCER

Hand of God
June 22, 1986: World Cup Quarterfinals, England vs. Argentina

When John F. Kennedy referenced the "hand of God" during his inaugural address in 1961, he was talking about gifts bestowed by a gracious God. When Mother Teresa said, "We are all pencils in the hand of God," she was referring to a guiding and protecting God. But at the 1986 World Cup, when Diego Maradona gave the "hand of God" credit for his opening goal in the quarterfinals, English soccer fans interpreted it as the work of the Old Testament, fire-and-brimstone, planet-destroying-floods God.

Maradona's exact quote in describing what stands as the most controversial goal in World Cup history was, "Un poco con la cabeza de Maradona y otro poco con la mano de Dios (a little with the head of Maradona and a little with the hand of God)."

The English-Argentine rivalry grew its roots at the 1966 World Cup when England defeated Argentina 1-0. The match was combative, and became controversial when Argentine captain Antonio Rattin received a red card in the first half for

1986 World Cup Semifinals, England vs. Argentina: Diego Maradona's infamous "Hand of God" goal lifts Argentina to victory.

"violence of the tongue," as described by the German referee who, it should be noted, spoke no Spanish.

Incensed by the penalty, the insolent Rattin forced police to escort him from the pitch and is then believed to have furthered his protest by staging a sit-in on the Queen's red carpet. In response to that insult to the Crown, England manager Alf Ramsey prevented his players from participating in the traditional postgame jersey swap, calling the Argentines "animals."

Throw in the three-month Falklands War of 1982, and you got yourself an intercontinental football rivalry.

The shame about Maradona's controversial goal in '86, other than the fact that it unfairly sent England to defeat in the quarterfinals, is that it completely overshadows his second goal of the game four minutes later, a brilliant up-field run through no less than six English defenders that was declared by the Fédération Internationale de Football (FIFA) in 2002 as the greatest goal ever scored in a World Cup game.

On the controversial goal, with the quarterfinal match a scoreless tie at the 51st minute, English midfielder Steve Hodge played a lazy ball back to goalkeeper Peter Shilton. But before Shilton could come up to meet the ball and knock it away, the speedy Maradona caught up to the play, coming up just short on the header with his 5' 6" frame but compensating by reaching up to punch the ball into the back of the net with his hand.

The surreptitious move, however, was not so sneaky. It was a clear handball, seen by every one of the 114,000 fans packing Mexico City's Estadio Azteca. Even the Argentine players held off on the celebration, knowing that the score would not be allowed.

"I was waiting for my teammates to embrace me and no one came," remembered Maradona years later. "I told them, come hug me or the referee isn't going to allow it."

Be it bad eyesight by the ref or good acting by the Argentine star, Tunisian referee Al Bennaceur did allow it, setting off heated protests from Shilton and the entire English bench, and unwittingly creating a legend that so voraciously invaded pop culture as to inspire countless songs and an animated re-creation of the play by Homer Simpson years later.

Bennaceur's blindness also had the minor effect of helping to propel Argentina to a 2-1 win and the eventual World Cup championship.

The England-Argentina rivalry continued with a controversial red card to David Beckham at the 1998 World Cup (an Argentina win on penalty kicks), and a questionable and decisive penalty kick awarded to the English at the 2002 World Cup (a 1-0 win for England).

But all other alleged interventions by the deity attenuate to the might of the "Hand of God."

Wembley Goal

July 30, 1966: World Cup Finals, England vs. West Germany

Before you start crying in your Earl Grey tea for England and its World Cup woes of 1986, let's not forget what happened *for* them in 1966, and on their home pitch of London's Wembley Stadium. There were conspiracy theories, rumors of World War II retribution, and a controversial deciding goal in the finals that underscores the value of high school geometry.

From the files of "strange bedfellows," and from the jilted South American nations who for the first time since 1934 failed to advance a team to the semifinals, came the conspiracy theory.

Argentina was knocked out by England with the aid of a West German referee. Uruguay was beaten by the Germans with a British referee presiding. And Brazil, the defending champs who failed to make it past the first round, was allegedly also undone by referees from the UK. This series of events, according to the Southern Hemisphere washouts, was obviously the work of a match-fixing partnership between West Germany and England.

A ridiculous notion when you consider that the scars of World War II were still visible in much of London, and scores of unhappy Germans had been created by FIFA's decision to pass over their bid for the 1966 tournament. But not so ridiculous that England didn't take the ensuing protests and abusive phone calls to its South American embassies seriously.

In a cable sent from the British Foreign Office to each of its embassies' information officers, the Brits admitted that an effort to mitigate the bad press by commissioning rebuttal articles from members of the foreign media had failed to bear fruit. And it was ultimately decided that any efforts by the British to argue their side would only prolong the protestors' emotions.

Ironically it was these same conjectured confederates, England and Germany, who met each other for one of the most memorable World Cup finals in history.

The world, and the 96,000 crazed English soccer fans who packed Wembley Stadium, were treated to a frenetically paced end-to-end game. The Germans scored first, the English tied it a short time later, and then took the lead late in the game, only to see the Germans tie it up 2-2 in the 90th and final minute. For the first time ever a World Cup final was going to extra time, ultimately birthing one of soccer's timeless controversies.

Some say that Russian linesman Tofik Bakhramov was getting back at Germany for World War II, or for West Germany's ouster of the Soviet Union in the semifinals. Bakhramov, however, wrote in his memoirs that his lifelong infamy was due to misjudgment, and nothing more.

Eleven minutes into extra time, England's Geoff Hurst received a cross from Alan Ball and fired it high at the German net, hitting the underside of the crossbar. The ball bounced straight down—apparently on or just over the goal line—and then bounced clear of the goal.

Swiss referee Gottfried Dienst had no idea where the ball hit, calling on his linesman for assistance. And in the judgment of Bakhramov, who would later have the national stadium of Azerbaijan named for him, the ball was in and the goal was good.

Up 3-2, and with the Germans desperately trying to score an equalizer in the final moments of extra time, England's Hurst added another goal to make it a 4-2 final score, claiming England's first and only World Cup title, and beginning years of controversy and the now four-decade-old rivalry between Germany and England.

In 1995, almost thirty years later, a group of researchers at Oxford University did a complex computer video analysis of Hurst's winning goal, concluding that without a doubt the ball did not cross the line and was therefore not a goal.

And proving that when wounded sports fans are involved, memories are forever, in 2006 when the Germans hosted the World Cup, an information Web site was published to assist the more than 100,000 English fans that made the trip to Germany. The site featured a series of important German phrases to know, including "Ihm war kotzuebel" (He was sick as a parrot), "Er kotzte wie ein Reiher" (He puked his guts up), and "Wembley-tor" (Wembley goal)—the phrase used to this day in Germany to describe all controversial goals.

Red-Handed Referees
June 9 to July 9, 2006: World Cup

What can we say about the refereeing at the 2006 World Cup that hasn't already been said? Gosh, it was really sorta kinda subpar?

In a word, it was dreadful. As nineteenth-century Scottish writer Thomas Carlyle once wrote, "Nothing is more terrible than activity without insight."

And that is exactly what the referees that were charged with patrolling the pitches of Germany were guilty of: assessing the two most punitive penalties in all of sports—the penalty kick and red card—without full cognizance that their actions, born from fallible judgment, may very well cost a team the championship.

First, let's address the red card. It not only knocks the offending player from the game, leaving his team a man down for the remainder of the contest, the red card automatically disqualifies him for the following match. Even the most egregious of personal fouls in the NFL don't penalize a team or player as much. When a hockey player is penalized for fighting, he's allowed to play the very next game. And after a basketball player collects his maximum number of fouls, the slate is wiped clean the next night.

In soccer, however, yellow and red cards follow a player for the entire tournament. And at the World Cup, when the first round is only three games long, and beyond that it's one loss and you're done, a player disqualification that stretches over multiple matches can have devastating effects for a club.

This, of course, has always been the case. The threat of the instant boot has hung over the heads of players since Cro-Magnon man first kicked a rock and called it football. But never before has the omnipotence of the officials so affected the field of play. At the 2006 Cup the referees pulled a record total of 28 red cards—a 27% increase in red cards over the previous record set in 1998. And that's to say nothing of English Premier League referee Graham Poll's lost count during the Croatia-Australia match, when he awarded a Croatian player three yellow cards instead of pulling a red after two.

Because of his mistake Poll was removed from the rest of the World Cup, prompting the contrite forty-two-year-old to retire from international competitions.

The worst-officiated match, by far, was the second-round meeting between Portugal and The Netherlands. During the ninety minutes of play, Russian referee Valentin Ivanov pulled an unheard of four red cards and sixteen yellows, bringing down upon him the wrath of the players, coaches, fans, and FIFA President Sepp Blather. In a shocking deviation from the normal support that FIFA showers its referees with, Blather said, "I consider that the referee was not at the same level as the players. There could have been a yellow card for the referee."

Actually, it turned out to be red. Following the controversial game, FIFA decided to drop Ivanov from the remainder of the tournament.

The penalty kick, which gives a player capable of kicking the ball 80 mph a direct shot at a 192-square-foot goal from 12 yards away, is essentially a free goal. And in a sport that is no stranger to 1-0 final scores, a free goal is often all it takes. Imagine if an intentional foul in basketball resulted in a 40-point play. That's basically what an awarded penalty kick does for the offensive team. And just like the red card, penalty kicks should be reserved for only the most severe of offenses.

Australia is no soccer world power. And it's unlikely that they will ever be confused for one. But in their second-round match against eventual champion Italy, the Socceroos hung with the Italians for ninety minutes, and for much of the game outplayed them. But in the closing moments of stoppage time, and mere seconds away from taking one of the pre-tournament favorite teams to overtime, the Aussies were undone by referee Luis Medina Cantelejo.

Italy's Fabio Grosso made the final push of the match, taking the ball on a desperation run into the Australian penalty box before falling to the ground between two defenders. It looked like he simply fell. At worst, Grosso was nudged off the ball by defender Lucas Neill, which of course is Neill's job. But Cantelejo (who in the tournament's final match was an off-field fourth official and the only one to witness the headbutt of Frenchman Zinedine Zidane) decided that Neill's action was nefarious enough to give Italy the game.

The penalty kick was called. Italy's Francesco Totti blasted home the game's first goal. And then seconds later, Cantelejo blew the whistle to end the match. Italy was the winner.

It was a terrible call made by a man with absolutely no concern for the fact that he personally was deciding the match. The Australians deserved better. And so did the hundreds of thousands of fans who made the journey to Germany, only to see their respective teams' fate ordained by erring officials.

AUTO RACING

500 Miles, Give or Take
June 7, 1997: True Value 500, Texas Motor Speedway

The elementary act of counting (1, 2, 3 . . .) has never been considered high-concept math. There's a simple reason Sesame Street's Count von Count is such a hit with four-year-olds. Simplicity. In fact, the very act of counting is considered so mundane that it has long been the preferred chemical-free cure for sleeplessness.

Of course, for every preschooler who can add apple slices, or insomniac who's found the sweet release of sleep through sheep tabulation, there is the image of a Floridian, squinting against the light, painstakingly assessing chads—pregnant and otherwise—and proving that counting isn't always straightforward.

And that takes us to the inaugural Indy Racing League event at Texas Motor Speedway, the True Value 500, and an infamous act by American racing legend A. J. Foyt.

Racing from the back of the pack because of a poor qualifying time, Foyt team driver Billy Boat ran an incredible race, eventually taking the checkered flag at the finish. But as the IRL was presenting the winner's trophy in Victory Lane to Foyt and the rookie Boat, Dutch driver Arie Luyendyk showed up to crash the party, claiming that he in fact had rightfully won the race.

Foyt, every bit as hot as his native Houston, didn't take too kindly to Luyendyk's intrusion, responding to the man who had just won the Indianapolis 500 with two punches to the back of the head. The sixty-two-year-old Foyt then grabbed Luyendyk around the neck and shoved him into a bed of tulips.

Foyt's paternal instinct to protect his team's moment of celebration, if not laughable, might be forgivable but for one small fact. Luyendyk was right. He had in fact won the race, but the United States Automobile Club's computerized scoring system (the IRL's sanctioning body until this specific incident) had failed to register two of Luyendyk's completed laps.

The following morning, after an all-night audit of the race's scoring revealed the discrepancy, the USAC upheld Luyendyk's protest by declaring him the winner and moving Boat to second place in the official standings. But when the IRL contacted Foyt to ask for the championship trophy back, he refused, saying, "We won the (expletive) race. We got the checkered flag."

And who could argue with that.

Apparently nobody. At least nobody had the cojones to. Foyt wasn't challenged further, with the IRL opting to take the anti-Solomon route by letting Foyt keep his trophy and awarding a duplicate to Luyendyk. They did, however, hit Foyt up for a $20,000 donation (fine) to the American Red Cross. Luyendyk had to contribute $14,000 for his role in The Tussle in the Tulips.

And because the forces of karma are always just, the unoffending Billy Boat, classy throughout in spite of his boss's example of defiance, recorded his first ever IRL win at this same race the very next year.

And that time it counted.

Chip Off the Old Rock

February 22, 2004: Subway 400, North Carolina Speedway

Ernest Hemingway (allegedly) said, "There are only three sports: bullfighting, motor racing, and mountaineering; all the rest are merely games."

And by further elimination, since two of this triumvirate of true sports don't include a governing body (unless you count goring horns and falling rocks), it stands to reason that as far as Papa was concerned, racing is the lone "civilized" sport. Of course, anyone who's spent a Sunday afternoon on the infield at Talladega or watched a heated "Ford vs. Chevy" dispute break into a bar fight might think that use of the word "civilized" is getting a little loose with the language.

And that goes double for anyone who's been grieved by the civilizing force behind stock car racing, NASCAR.

In this case, team owner Chip Ganassi, himself a former driver who competed five times in the Indianapolis 500 before an injury ended his career, is the aggrieved party, telling reporters after the 2004 Subway 400 at Rockingham, "We was robbed in front of 100,000 people with their eyes wide open."

The referenced robbery happened on lap 350, when drivers Matt Kenseth and Kasey Kahne, running one and two and just ahead of Ganassi's driver Jaime McMurray, decided to make their final pit stops of the day. As the two leaders pulled out of the field and onto pit road, McMurray cycled past the pair and moved into first place.

As new leader McMurray entered turn three, and while Kenseth and Kahne were still getting serviced, Robby Gordon slid into Jeff Green and into the outside wall to bring out the yellow caution flag. That also brought out the pace car, which proceeded to pick up the field of racers and pass the pitting former front runners before they could reenter the track.

That should have left Kenseth and Kahne a lap down, and McMurray in the lead. But for some reason, even though Kenseth and Kahne were off the track, had been passed by the field, and had failed to make it off pit road in time to beat the pace car, race officials determined that when the yellow caution came out and the field was frozen, they were still the leaders.

Kenseth and Kahne were given the unusual privilege of driving around the pace car during the caution, which put them back into the order in which they would eventually finish, just ahead of third-place finisher McMurray.

Felix Sabates, a minority owner of McMurray's car, echoed his boss's outrage, boldly claiming, "We won the race. [NASCAR] knows we won it, and so did everyone else here. But NASCAR is never going to admit they made a mistake."

Sabates then encapsulated the entire team's indignation with the withering witticism, "Sometimes you win, sometimes you get the shaft, and sometimes you get the elevator. We got the shaft."

Which leaves us wondering: "The elevator?"

GOLF

Ryder in the Storm
September 17, 1971: Nineteenth Ryder Cup, Day Two

American author and noted naturalist Henry David Thoreau once said, "Any fool can make a rule, and any fool will mind it."

Thoreau's famous work *Civil Disobedience*, and the multitude of ideas that were hatched from its pages, influenced a great many world thinkers. In his autobiography, Martin Luther King Jr. credited Thoreau as the "eloquent and passionate" patriarch of passive civil resistance. And Mohandas Gandhi actually thanked the American people for the New England philosopher, saying, "You have given me a teacher in Thoreau."

Thoreau's compartmentalization of "evil" laws, and the belief that an individual's conscience required him to disobey the rules that perpetrated injustice, changed the world. Just as blindly following said rules in the face of a commonsense lure to the contrary has the power to destroy it.

Or at the very minimum, take down a pretty good round of golf.

You'll be hard pressed to find a more impressive group of golfing greats than the anchors of the 1971 United States Ryder Cup team. Led by Jack Nicklaus, Arnold Palmer, Lee Trevino, and Billy Casper, the host Americans went to St. Louis in September with almost certain victory in their eyes, while the British traveled across the Atlantic resigned to near-predetermined assurances of defeat.

That feeling of a guaranteed result, however, didn't last long. The Britons were strong out of the gate on day one, picking up a pair of points against the team of Billy Casper and Miller Barber, as well as a 3-and-2 win over the Jack Nicklaus/Dave Stockton pairing. And when the first-day dust had settled at the

Old Warson Country Club, Great Britain was up 4½ to 3½ and threatening to win their first ever Ryder Cup on American soil.

With the United States trailing to begin day two, Arnold Palmer, already a four-time Ryder Cup winner (he would end his career with seven Cup wins and twenty-two match victories), and teammate Gardner Dickinson took the early lead in their important four-ball match against Peter Oosterhuis and Bernard Gallacher. After six holes Palmer and Dickinson led the Brits, 1-up.

With the honor on the 208-yard par-3 seventh hole, Palmer stepped up to the tee and whacked a beautiful shot into the heart of the green. In awe of the legend's play from the tee, Gallacher's caddie said, "Gee, Mr. Palmer. That was a terrific shot. What club did you hit?"

Palmer replied, "Five-iron."

It was a banal exchange that virtually no one on the course had any reason to give thought to. Anybody could look at what club Palmer was holding to see that it was a five. But that single innocuous question, followed by Palmer's confirmation of the observable, struck a chord with referee John Conley. He immediately recognized it as a violation of Rule 9a: "A player may give advice to, or ask for advice from, only his partner or either of their caddies."

The players continued to play the hole as if nothing had happened, because in their minds nothing had. And they ended up halving the hole at three strokes each. But as the four golfers continued their match to the eighth tee, Conley, after consulting with PGA Tour commissioner Joe Dey and PGA president Joe Black, ruled that the seventh hole had to be forfeited to the United States.

Never mind that Gallacher's caddie was an American college student who had no affiliation to either of the British players. Who cares that Gallacher didn't appear to hear the crimeless conversation born from curiosity, changing his original choice of a four-iron to a longer hitting three-iron, and clearly not benefiting from his caddie's knowledge of Palmer's five-iron. And it simply didn't matter that Palmer himself, who in theory was just as guilty for offering the "advice," asked the referee to keep the hole's result as it was played.

A rule had been broken, and a penalty must be paid.

The seventh-hole forfeiture put Gallacher and Oosterhuis down to the Americans by two, setting the stage for their collapse on the back nine and Palmer and Dickinson's 5-and-4 victory. And that helped accelerate a terrible day for the British team. The United States outscored their cousins from across the pond 6½ to 1½ on the second day of competition, eventually securing their fifteenth Ryder Cup win the following afternoon, 18½ to 13½, with dominant singles performances by Trevino (7-and-6) and Nicklaus (5-and-3).

Ironically, but in no way exacting a fair level of retribution for the British, both Gallacher and Oosterhuis won their day-three singles matches, while Palmer and Dickinson lost.

The golfing powers that be were right to have written such a detailed set of rules. But in this case, they were absolutely wrong in enforcing them in such a heavy-handed way that did nothing to protect their intent. Conley's ruling, backed by his superiors, served no one. But what it did do was pollute the American victory and stain an otherwise great weekend of history-making golf.

As Thoreau wrote in his well-known self-examination of civilization, *Walden*, "There is no odor so bad as that which arises from goodness tainted."

Amateur Standing

1914: U.S. Amateur Championship

Just as the legends of entertainment that adorn the Hollywood Walk of Fame go through a challenging and laborious nomination process that concludes with a required $15,000 donation to the

Hollywood Historic Trust, the sports world similarly weeds through its own checks and balances before settling on its select list of immortals.

First, there must be a book. A song, such as Count Basie's *Did You See Jackie Robinson Hit That Ball*, doesn't hurt. Poems are a plus, like Franklin Pierce Adams's *Tinker to Evers to Chance* (the largely unknown but correct title is *Baseball's Sad Lexicon*). And a candy bar is practically a shoe-in.

But for a free pass to the head of the line and immediate induction into the hall of sports legends, all an athlete really needs is Walt Disney. Or more specifically, Michael Eisner.

You may know Francis Ouimet as the main character of Disney's based-on-a-true-story *The Greatest Game Ever Played*. The reality is that before Tiger Woods, Arnold Palmer, or Ben Hogan, he was America's golf hero. Ouimet was the golfer that wowed galleries and inspired young players, and has often been called the "Father of Amateur Golf."

He also might be called the amateur that almost wasn't, if the United States Golf Association (USGA) had gotten its way.

As a twenty-year-old amateur and former caddie, Francis Ouimet shocked the world and the golfing greats from England and Scotland—who to date hadn't received much competition from Americans—by winning the 1913 U.S. Open. He took the championship in an 18-hole playoff over experienced Britons Harry Vardon and Ted Ray, who between them would finish their careers with nine major championships.

The following year, Ouimet added the U.S. Amateur Championship to his trophy chest of feats.

Having started a golfing revolution in the working-class neighborhoods that bore him, and being fully committed to making the sport available to everyone (prior to his Open win in 1913, the United States had no public courses), Ouimet capitalized on the U.S. Amateur title and used his growing fame to open his own sporting-goods store.

We certainly don't want to accuse the powers that be of pandering to their firmly entrenched old boys' network. Or imply that they were doing anything untoward, like trying to dispense with Ouimet and the "lower class undesirables" he was inspiring to take up their country-club pastime. But the scornfully stodgy USGA ruled that Ouimet's sporting-goods store was akin to him turning pro, and the governing body promptly stripped the young champion of his amateur standing.

In defense of the USGA's apparent malfeasance, this was the age of idiocy in the association. If a person was paid to caddie, and was over the age of fourteen, he was a professional golfer. So in the case of Ouimet's ban, perhaps zeal was at play and not prejudice.

Whatever the motive, the result was the same. Ouimet was no longer an amateur. He, of course, would fight this. And popular opinion among his fans and peers was largely in his favor. But the USGA held firm to its miscarriage of justice, denying Ouimet's appeal and keeping him off the course.

Luckily in the end the USGA's stubbornness subsided and intelligent heads prevailed, and Ouimet had his amateur status restored in 1918—a historically significant decision, as it turned out.

Beginning with its inception in 1922, Ouimet played on the first eight Walker Cup teams and captained the following four, compiling an overall record of 11-1. In 1931 he captured a second U.S. Amateur championship. And in 1951 Ouimet became the first American and non-Briton elected captain of the Royal and Ancient Golf Club of St. Andrews.

In 1995 the saga came full circle when the famous image of Ouimet at the 1913 U.S. Open with ten-year-old caddie Eddie Lowery was selected as the logo for the USGA's centennial celebration.

And the USGA itself nearly prevented all of that from happening.

Big Easy Lie
June 19, 1994: U.S. Open, Oakmont Country Club

There is no regulating body in sports, or otherwise, that is as psychotically anal about its rules as is the USGA. The USGA treats rules as unbreakable laws written by the hand of God. Failure to correctly assess penalty strokes or properly execute a ball drop is considered obscene in the eye of the keepers of the game. And playing out of turn and grounding your club are both considered floggable offenses.

And that's why so many years later, the 1994 U.S. Open at Oakmont is still a USGA embarrassment.

Ernie Els, by all accounts one of the most affable golfers on the PGA tour, was lucky just to be in the field at Oakmont. The year before, at Baltusrol, Els played in the Open on a USGA exemption, and would have missed the cut on Friday had Lee Janzen not missed a putt on the 36th hole. But Els survived, made the most of his good fortune by playing his way to a top-10 finish, and qualified for the Open the following year.

Considering that an American had won the previous twelve U.S. Opens, and Ernie Els had yet to win on the PGA Tour, the South African wasn't given much of a chance to win in '94. But on Sunday, The Big Easy, nicknamed for his 6-foot-3 frame, effortless swing, and easygoing manner, went into the final 18 holes with a two-stroke lead.

Teeing off to start the fourth and final round, Els hooked his drive into the deep rough down the left side of the fairway. In the words of Bob Rosburg, ABC's on-course reporter, it was "one of the worst lies I've ever seen." But it also happened to lie behind a giant television crane. And because of that, USGA official Trey Holland ruled that Els was entitled to "line-of-sight" relief.

Holland determined, incorrectly, that the crane was an immovable object. In fact, it had already been moved four times that day, it was moved later in the day to provide overhead

1994 U.S. Open: Ernie Els wins his first U.S. Open after an official incorrectly gives him a drop in the final round.

shots for other holes on the course, and it had been outlined as "movable" in ABC's pre-tournament plans made available to every USGA official.

So Els's second shot, instead of coming in what he described as "grass up to my waist," came from a patch of long rough that had been hard-packed by the 25,000-strong gallery of fans. And because of that improved and considerably easier lie, Els was able to land the ball on the green and finish the hole with a bogey-five.

Els would later admit that if he'd been forced to play the ball from the original spot, as the rules say he should have, "it could have been a double, or even more."

Without those saved strokes Els doesn't shoot a 72 and finish the round in a three-way tie with Loren Roberts and Colin Montgomerie. Therefore he's not around for Monday's playoff, which, of course, he won. The 1994 U.S. Open title, instead of being Els's first, would have gone to either Roberts (the second-place finisher) or Montgomerie, two golfers who to this day have never won a major championship.

A distinction that both men say, somewhat unconvincingly, no longer bothers them.

There is a thread to this story, however, that goes beyond blunder.

This was the era of the armchair judge. In 1991 Paul Azinger was disqualified at Doral after a television viewer in Colorado called the PGA to report a rules violation. A similar ruling by remote control happened a year later at the Dutch Heineken Open. And because of those two troubling events, golf began assigning a keeper of the rules to monitor all television broadcasts.

According to USGA Executive Director David Fay, former colleague and then-ABC-broadcaster Frank Hannigan held that job at Oakmont in 1994. Fay called it their "fail-safe."

But obviously it failed to work, either by bad luck or bad blood.

Hannigan says that he could only advise the USGA about a rules violation during a commercial break. And between the time of the ruling, Els's free drop, and the ensuing improper and controversial second shot, there wasn't one. A fact that Reg Murphy, then the USGA president, claims was no accident.

Two weeks prior to Oakmont the USGA had awarded its future television rights to NBC, making ABC a very unhappy lame-duck network. And both Murphy and Fay have said that because of its bitterness, ABC not only didn't lend a helping hand when it could have, it went out of its way to embarrass the USGA. ABC producers naturally called that charge "nonsense."

Whatever the forces at play here were—misstep, misjudgment,

or malevolence—everyone agrees, including the beneficiary himself, that Ernie Els was given an awfully big break.

The Schenectady
1904: British Amateur Championship

Golf, more than any other sport that takes place outside a race car, is ruled by its equipment. Graphite vs. steel. Firm vs. flexible. Keel sole vs. deep face. Soft cover vs. solid core. Plaid pants vs. plain chinos.

To hear the pro golfers tell it, every minor change in equipment can have major effects on the course. Remember the hubbub that surrounded Tiger Woods's change to Nike Forged Irons in 2003? And his incredible run in 2005, when he won both The Masters and British Open, finished second at the U.S. Open, and fourth at the PGA Championship, was directly attributed to his switch that year to the Nike One Platinum golf ball.

At least, it was by Nike.

But no club change or newly manufactured golf ball has ever caused the stir that Walter Travis's putter did in 1904.

Travis should serve as an inspiration to hackers across America. In four short years, and in his late thirties, Travis went from a brand-new golfer to U.S. Amateur champion. And by the time he made the transatlantic trip to Sandwich, England, for the British Amateur in 1904, he had won the American equivalent three times in four years.

Travis's key to success was hard work and innovative equipment. He experimented with a 52-inch driver, more than half a foot longer than what was standard at the time. In 1902 he adopted a wound ball while most other golfers stayed loyal to the ball made out of gutta-percha latex. And by the time Travis made his journey to take on the Brits, he was using a newly designed center-shafted putter.

The "Schenectady"—named for the upstate New York hometown of its creator, General Electric engineer Arthur F. Knight—broke from convention by taking the connection between the shaft and head, until then at the head's heel, and moving it closer to the center. And it was that design that helped Travis master the art of putting and dominate the difficult greens in England.

Travis was old, forty-three, short off the tee, and an American. And he had just come to England and beaten the British at their own game. That combination didn't sit well with the keepers of golf, the Royal and Ancient Golf Club Committee on the Rules of Golf (their official title, really), and thus his putter was determined to be too much like a croquet mallet and therefore illegal in golf.

Breaking form, the USGA uncharacteristically refused to recognize the R&A's sour grapes ruling, keeping the putter legal in the United States. So while Travis could use and endorse the putter at home, which he did, he couldn't go back to Britain and try to win again—which he had no real desire to do after the shoddy treatment he'd received there in 1904.

Bob Labbance, the author of Travis's biography *The Old Man*, said that Travis was refused a room at the player's hotel, wasn't given a locker to use at the course, and tournament officials stuck him with the area's worst caddie. And all of that left Travis with a sour taste in his mouth that couldn't be attributed to notorious English cooking.

In 1952, nearly five decades after the center-shafted putter had become the norm in the United States, the Royal and Ancient finally lifted its ban. Twenty-five years after its most famous user had passed away.

BOXING

Tunney's Long Count
September 22, 1927: Jack Dempsey vs. Gene Tunney

When it comes to sports icons and enduring American legends, no decade in history holds a candle to the 1920s.

Babe Ruth redefined the home run's place in baseball, increasing the all-time mark by more than 400%. Golfer Bobby Jones won thirteen major championships, including a first, and to this day only, sweep of all four grand-slam tournaments. Red Grange was a three-time All-American at Illinois, making it to the cover of *Time* magazine in 1925. And boxing boasted the great Jack Dempsey, the holder of the world heavyweight title from 1919 until he was beaten by Gene Tunney in 1926 in Philadelphia.

In the rematch a year later in 1927, a legendary sports controversy was born.

In front of 104,000 fight fans packed into Chicago's Soldier Field (paying a then-record gate of more than $2.6 million, a record that stood for fifty years), and with another 50 million fans across the country listening to the radio broadcast, the two fighters met in the most anticipated rematch in boxing history.

Dempsey was a colorful legend and a man of the people. He was the "Manassa Mauler," a salt-of-the-earth product of Colorado mining and lumber camps who regularly treated boxing writers to free drinks and practical jokes. Tunney, on the other hand, was a disciplined boxer and former Marine from New York's Greenwich Village. Gentleman Gene was reserved and educated, a reader of Shakespeare, and thus considered an outsider by the 1920s boxing mob.

Years later, though, these two disparate men would be known as bonded friends. Dempsey and Tunney campaigned together to get Tunney's son John elected to the U.S. Congress in 1964.

September 22, 1927: While the referee tries to get Jack Dempsey to a neutral corner Jim Tunney gets a 14-second count.

And in 1978, when the elder Tunney passed away, Dempsey said, "I feel like a part of me is gone."

It was a faithful five-decade relationship forged by an infamous 15-second moment that September night in Chicago.

The early rounds of the bout were uneventful. Dempsey, showing much more respect for his opponent than he did the year before, patiently waited for his chance to strike. Tunney calmly worked his jabs and crosses, opening a series of cuts over Dempsey's eyes by the fifth.

By the seventh round, just as he had in Philadelphia to take the title, Tunney was well ahead of Dempsey on points. But points weren't how Dempsey, who is said to have recorded twenty-six career unconscious first-round knockouts, won his fights.

Fifty seconds into the seventh round, and after Tunney hit Dempsey with a straight right hand, Dempsey countered with a right to the head and a left hook directly on the chin, sending Tunney slumping to the canvas for the first time in his career.

The 1927 knockdown rule of the Illinois State Athletic Commission was very clear. When a knockdown occurs, the timekeeper shall immediately begin counting the seconds. And once the referee puts the opponent in the furthest corner *he shall pick up the count in unison with the timekeeper.*

Dempsey, not used to the new rule requiring a boxer to wait out the count in a neutral corner, initially didn't respond to referee Dave Barry's orders. Dempsey had made a career out of waiting near a fallen fighter and pouncing once he'd regained his feet, and that was exactly what he was hoping to do to Tunney.

Finally Dempsey was coaxed into a neutral corner, and Barry (a last-minute replacement referee after it was rumored that Al Capone was trying to fix the fight) turned to the fallen Tunney. But instead of picking up timekeeper Paul Beeler's count, already up to five, Barry began a new count at one—violating the Commission's rules.

When Barry's count reached nine, 14 seconds after Tunney went down, the champion got up and recovered enough to survive the round. He then went on to take the fight in a unanimous decision, retaining the title, and effectively ending Dempsey's storied boxing career.

There are many who claim that even if Barry's count had been correct, Tunney would have survived the knockdown. He was an intelligent fighter who was simply waiting, and recovering, until the count's final second.

But in the words of ringsider Arthur Daley, working the fight for *The New York Times*, "When Tunney hit the deck he was out. His eyes were glazed." Judge George Lytton, one of the men who gave the decision to Tunney, said, "There have been many remarks to the effect that Tunney could have risen sooner. I don't think so."

And then there is Tunney himself, who years later would admit that as he was standing up on the count of nine, he wasn't sure if his legs could hold him.

Does that sound like a man collected, waiting out the count?

Dempsey, for his part, always defended his friend, placing the blame on his own failure to quickly find a neutral corner. But despite the assertions of the principal parties involved, this timeless debate rages on.

Thunder Meets Lightning
March 17, 1990: Meldrick Taylor vs. Julio Cesar Chavez

In no other sport does a losing top-ranked contender get thrown to the scrapheap of also-rans faster than boxing. In less than an hour a fighter can go from a champion's promise to pitiful washout. It's what Thomas Moore described as fleeting glory followed by eternal obscurity.

Although in the case of Meldrick Taylor's ruination, eternal obscurity was accompanied by unremitting torment.

Taylor had everything a fighter needed to be a great world champion. He hailed from Philadelphia (home to more than two dozen past title holders, including Joe Frazier and Rocky Balboa), he was an Olympic gold medalist before the age of eighteen, and by twenty-two, after beating James "Buddy" McGirt, he was the International Boxing Federation's (IBF) world junior welterweight champion.

But one rather large obstacle stood between Taylor and the title of "world champion"—the legendary Julio Cesar Chavez, whose final résumé boasted eighty career knockouts, five world titles in three weight classes, and a short but much envied romantic relationship with Salma Hayek.

The younger and faster Taylor entered the St. Patrick's Day unification bout with the more experienced and harder-punching

Chavez an undefeated 24-0-1. Chavez was an eye-popping 68-0, and favored to run his streak to 69 straight.

Like in any storm, the lightning came before the thunder. The quicker Taylor was all over Chavez, controlling the fight and pushing his older opponent around the ring. For every punch Chavez was able to land, Taylor countered with three or four connecting blows. But as the fight progressed and Taylor continued to rack up rounds, Chavez's thunderous punches began to do their damage.

But it seemed like it was too little, too late for Chavez. Entering the 12th and final round, while the shaken Taylor's face was swollen and battered, he was also the consensus leader. HBO had the score a near shutout in favor of Taylor, and as everyone would find out after the fight, he had big leads on two of the three judges' scorecards.

The fight was classic, the final round a war, and the final seconds are some of the most debated in boxing history. With just 15 seconds to go, a huge right hand from Chavez sent Taylor sprawling to the floor. Taylor made it back to his feet at referee Richard Steele's count of five. But as he was looking past Steele to his corner for instructions, he missed Steele, who had just completed the mandatory eight-count, asking, "Are you okay?"

Steele asked a second time, "Are you okay?" But before Taylor could do little more than nod, Steele inexplicably, outrageously, and unforgivably immediately stopped the fight.

Just 2 seconds remained.

After 11 rounds, 2 minutes, and 58 seconds, Chavez was the winner by TKO.

The scorecards were 108-101 for Taylor, 107-102 for Taylor, and 105-104 for Chavez. In this case we don't have to ask "what if" Steele hadn't stopped the fight. We know. Taylor would have beaten one of the greatest fighters in history, and the sky would have been his limit. Instead, as the loser, he was never the same fighter, or man, again.

Taylor went up in weight class a year later and won the welterweight title from Aaron Davis. But when he finally got his rematch with Chavez, Taylor was the loser in eight rounds.

Steele's critics—and there were many—say that knowing that there were less than ten seconds remaining in the fight (red lights were on in each corner to alert him), he should have absolutely let a world championship fight be decided by the fighters themselves. Taylor was on his feet and just ticks of the clock remained.

But Steele's defenders, a group pretty much limited to him and supporters of Chavez, say he did the right thing. And the sad state of Taylor's deteriorating coherence since 1990 is evidence that he was badly beaten, in serious danger, and in need of a referee's rescue.

Maybe. But waiting two more seconds, while having no adverse effect on Taylor's health, would have most definitely changed his life.

TENNIS

Sprem Donation
June 24, 2004: Wimbledon 2nd Round,
Venus Williams vs. Karolina Sprem

You knew it was only a matter of time before there would be a counting error in tennis. We are, after all, talking about a sport that plays games to four, yet counts those points as 15, 30, and 40 (isn't 45 next in the sequence?). Then, when the score is tied 40-40 (really 3-3), the chair umpire inexplicably calls out *Deuce!*, which signifies the number two to anyone familiar with a deck of cards, dice games, bathroom humor, or Patrick Swayze films (see *Roadhouse*).

And let's not forget that in tennis *love* means *zero*, which surely says something about how Frenchmen felt about their wives in the early 1500s, the time and place that most tennis terms are believed to have originated.

And all of that takes us across the channel to the All England Lawn Tennis and Croquet Club, the site of the Wimbledon Championships.

Venus Williams entered Wimbledon in 2004 having appeared in the finals for four straight years, winning in 2000 and 2001 and finishing as a runner-up to her sister Serena in 2002 and 2003. So Venus's second-round match in '04 against Croatian Karolina Sprem, the 30th-ranked player in the world, seemed like nothing more than a blip on the radar. But that blip turned into a mistakenly awarded point, and an improbable straight-sets loss.

In the second, and ultimately deciding set tiebreaker, and with Williams up 2-1, Sprem's first serve was ruled wide by the line judge with a call of "Fault!" Williams, obviously having heard the judge, nonchalantly hit the ball back over the net, and Sprem returned it into the open court.

But as the players lined up for a second-service, chair umpire Ted Watts announced the score as 2-2, obviously missing the line judge's call and erroneously awarding Sprem a point.

Both players would later confess that they had heard Watts's incorrect call. But both of them said that they often get so locked in during a match that they lose track of the score. Watts, however, should have been alerted to the mistake, or at least to confusion among the players, when Sprem and Williams lined up for a second serve on the same side of the court.

He was not. And when Williams returned that serve of Sprem's for a backhand winner, Watts called the score 3-2 for Williams, when it should have been 3-1. And once the players had played that point, said tournament referee Alan Mills, there was no going back. A protest must be lodged at the time the mistake is made.

Williams would push her lead in the tiebreaker to as much as 6-3, but Sprem was able to rally. And with the aid of the extra point she was able to take the tiebreaker 8-6, win the match in straight sets, and send Venus Williams to her earliest defeat at Wimbledon since 1997. Venus, to her credit, never blamed the referee for the defeat.

Watts was relieved of his umpiring duties for the remainder of the Fortnight, and for the first time in three years the Wimbledon final was not an all-Williams family affair.

And in the ultimate of silver linings, Venus's early ouster helped usher in the era of Maria Sharapova, the eventual 2004 Wimbledon champion that had men across the world asking, "Anna Kournikova who?"

Flushing Serena
September 7, 2004: U.S. Open Quarterfinals,
Jennifer Capriati vs. Serena Williams

Two and a half months after sister Venus was ousted from a Grand Slam tournament with the aid of an umpire, Serena Williams met a similar fate at the U.S. Open in Flushing Meadows while playing Jennifer Capriati. Instead of the inadvertent brain cramp by Ted Watts, chair umpire Mariana Alves proved to be an inflexible egotist in a match that was too far above her pay grade.

The root of the problem that befell Serena began growing at the 2004 Athens Olympics, which had just celebrated its closing ceremonies nine days earlier. During the U.S. Open's early rounds, three of tennis's so-called gold-badge chair umpires had been dismissed for their roles in a credential-forging scheme in Athens. According to the *New York Daily News*, during the Olympics the judges in question had altered their credentials to allow themselves increased access to the Game's venues. And two

2004 U.S. Open Quarterfinals, Serena Williams vs. Jennifer Capriati: A stunned Serena demands to know why chair umpire Mariana Alves overruled the line judge.

of those officials had actually been deported by Greek authorities after they tried to pass off the forgeries as legitimate.

Because the Open was now short-handed in the chair, Alves, just a "silver-badge" judge, was not only uncharacteristically working a quarterfinals match between two of tennis's top players, she was working a show court match for a fifth straight day. According to an umpire who spoke to the *Daily News* anonymously, "Even working back-to-back days on a show court is unusual."

Maybe she was simply worn out from being overworked. Perhaps she knew that she was in over her head. Whatever the reason, Alves's actions and subsequent behavior in the opening game of the third set were inexcusable.

With game one at deuce, Serena smacked a clear backhand

winner, ruled "in" by the line judge and without a question from Capriati, down the side of the court opposite from where the umpire sits. But as Serena turned her back on the play and made her way back to the baseline for her advantage, Alves inexplicably overruled the call, announcing, "Advantage, Capriati."

Stunned, Serena turned to the umpire and demanded to know why she would overrule a call so far out of her sight line. And when Serena didn't get a satisfactory answer to that question, she asked Alves to consult with the ruling line judge. But the unflinching and unwilling Alves refused, threatening Serena with a stop-arguing-or-else.

Capriati went on to win the critical first game, and with the help of two other questionable calls that can't be pinned exclusively on Alves, she went on to take the set and match, and advance to the semifinals.

Replays clearly showed that Serena was robbed. And when one of your top draws is wronged on your sport's biggest stage, you try to make things right. Tournament referee Brian Earley admitted the error, and announced the next day that Alves wouldn't work another match at the 2004 U.S. Open. And Arlen Kantarian, the chief executive of Professional Tennis, took the unusual step of personally calling Serena to apologize.

Unlike her sister had been in June, Serena was not so judicious. Nor was she quieted by the official admission of wrongdoing. "I am very angry and bitter right now," said Serena after the match. "I feel cheated and robbed. I'd prefer [Alves] not umpire my court anymore. She's obviously anti-Serena."

Serena's father Richard Williams took the accusation a step further, crying conspiracy and racism, and saying, "I really think the umpire was prejudiced."

To be fair to Alves, there is absolutely no evidence that there was anything more sinister at play other than the umpire's own incompetence. Which, of course, doesn't make the end result any fairer for Serena Williams.

Tape-Measure Turmoil
April 8, 2002: Bausch & Lomb Championships 1st Round,
Jennifer Hopkins vs. Anne Kremer

Every sports fan knows that a football field is 100 yards long. It's 90 feet between bases on a baseball diamond. Baskets are hung 10 feet above the basketball court. And NHL ice rinks are 200 by 85 feet. Perhaps you didn't know that last one, since the rink grows fatter in international play, and outside of the NHL's specifications, sometimes the exact dimensions have to conform to the arena.

But can anyone name the dimensions of a tennis court? Don't worry, you're not alone. In fact, your ignorance might qualify you to be the head groundskeeper at the Amelia Island Plantation racquet park.

Bert Evatt, by all accounts a respected and competent groundskeeper, held the position in 2002, his twenty-second year on the job. And no doubt until April 8 of that year most people outside the park or not employed by the Women's Tennis Association (WTA) had never heard his name. But that all changed with an embarrassing gaffe in arithmetic of overhand-smash proportions.

As he had done every year the week prior to the start of the WTA's Bausch & Lomb Championships, Evatt resurfaced and relined the courts. After twenty-one years of contouring, constructing, and coating, it's probably safe to say that the task had become monotonous. Or at the very least, uneventful. Evatt had grown used to the routines of his springtime duty and to date had completed it flawlessly.

The following day the tournament started, and problems appeared immediately. Jennifer Hopkins and Anne Kremer had the honor (misfortune) of playing the stadium court first. And both came out of the gates with extremely sloppy play and an inordinate number of double faults.

Both players complained to the chair umpire that something

wasn't right. And Hopkins actually went so far as to ask the umpire to stop the match and measure the court, convinced that somehow the dimensions of the surface were off. But he ignored their intuition and told the players to stop complaining and play. They did, and eventually bumbled their way to a disastrous twenty-nine double faults during the three-set Kremer win.

With the break in the action between matches, tournament officials finally decided to take the measurements that the players had been lobbying for. And guess what, the players were right. Instead of 21 feet between the net and service line, and then 18 feet back to the baseline, those numbers were reversed, giving the players 3 less feet than normal to place their serves—accounting for the high number of double faults.

Too many times tennis officials have hidden behind the defense, *if only the player had protested*. Well, this time they did, both of them, multiple times, and no one bothered to listen. And that allowed a mistake that was simple to discover and even easier to correct (move them to another court) to alter the outcome of a tournament.

For his role in the debacle, Bert Evatt couldn't apologize enough, taking full responsibility for the error and telling reporters, "I screwed up. I measured them wrong. I've been lining these courts for twenty-two years, have done it hundreds of times, and have never messed it up like this before."

And you can be sure that now each spring those line measurements are double and triple checked, and then checked again.

As for what to do with the hopping-mad Hopkins, who had unjustly double-faulted her way out of the tournament, the WTA deliberated for nearly six hours on whether or not the match should be replayed. But in the end they opted to hide this time behind the *an umpire's decision is final* defense.

CYCLING

French Dopes
1999–2005 Tour de France

If, as it is said, arrogance is a kingdom without a crown, then World Anti-Doping Agency (WADA) chairman Dick Pound is truly an emperor without clothes. Or at the very least, one who is so preoccupied by his policing fiefdom that he is now indifferent to trivial matters like evidence and truth.

No athlete has ever more thoroughly dominated an endurance sport for a longer period of time than Lance Armstrong did the Tour de France. During his record-setting seven consecutive wins, Armstrong won twenty-five stages and time trials, and captured his trophy case full of yellow jerseys by a combined time of more than thirty-nine minutes.

The problem for Armstrong—and why after surviving cancer, winning four Associated Press Male Athlete of the Year awards, and making the world's most grueling event his own personal playground, he still doesn't get his due worldwide—is that his workmanlike dominance offends European dominion in what has been called the world's most drug-soaked sport.

Europeans have been cheating for years, entire teams have been suspended, and doctors have been arrested. They simply can't believe that a brash Texan could come in and destroy their record book with clean blood. Never mind that in seven years of intense drug testing he never once tested positive. And as the spotlight of suspicion sharpened, reducing his opportunities to cheat with impunity to nearly nonexistent, Armstrong only got faster.

The writers of *L'Équipe*, a Paris-based sports daily and self-appointed Woodward and Bernstein of the Tour (the paper created the Tour de France in 1903 to increase circulation), published an article in 2005 called *"Le Mensonge Armstrong"* ("The

Armstrong Lie"). Since Armstrong won his first Tour in 1999, the French, including many race officials, have publicly questioned the legitimacy of his wins. But *L'Équipe* investigative journalist (cough, cough) Damien Ressiot claimed to have definitive proof that Armstrong was the biggest fraud perpetrated on the public since the Ab Energizer.

Ressiot said, "The facts are indisputable." He compared anonymous urine sample tests conducted by a French lab with identifying numbers from control reports that allegedly named Armstrong. And according to the article, the samples, from 1999 and frozen for five years before they were tested, showed traces of the red blood cell booster EPO.

Ressiot further alleged that his sources for the information identifying Armstrong came from inside the Union Cycliste Internationale (UCI), the sanctioning body of professional cycling.

The motives of Ressiot were immediately questioned, and the legality of his methods investigated by French police. The accuracy of the five-year-old test with no chain of custody was also questioned, as was the legitimacy of a single sample positive, which has never been enough in any sport in any country to allow for an athlete to be sanctioned.

An independent investigation by Dutch attorney Emile Vrijman, commissioned by the UCI and released a year later, declared it "completely irresponsible" to suggest *L'Équipe*'s tests "constitute evidence of anything." Vrijman, who for ten years was in charge of Holland's anti-doping agency, also said his report "exonerates Lance Armstrong completely."

So, where do you suppose the officials of the UCI, the Tour de France, and the WADA were during the Armstrong Salem witch trials? Aligned firmly against their star athlete, of course.

Tour director Jean-Marie Leblanc said of the man who single-handedly made it cool to wear yellow, "We were all fooled by Armstrong." Pound said the WADA has "completely rejected" the report written by Vrijman and would consider legal action against "any organization, including UCI, that may publicly adopt its conclusions." And running scared from the vengeful and litigious Pound, the UCI, unhappy that Vrijman released his findings without clearing it with them first, said they "firmly deplore" the independent investigator's behavior.

Apparently the word "independent" doesn't translate well into French.

In the wake of the shockwaves that were sent through the Tour in 2006—with the pre-race suspensions of favorites Jan Ullrich and Ivan Basso and the postrace revelation that first-place finisher Floyd Landis had failed a drug test after stage 17, taking him from celebrated conqueror to contemptible castaway faster than you can say *au revoir*—we know that drug testing at the Tour de France, while not perfect, works.

But despite the consistent denials that he ever took drugs, repeated drug tests under the intensity of suspicion, and absolutely no evidence that could be considered a legitimate positive test, the very people who should care most about the truth continue to presume Armstrong guilty.

He's just that good. Or they're just that pigheaded.

CURLING

Prozac, Eh?
March 9, 2002: Quebec vs. Manitoba

Roman historian Titus Livius penned, "Greater is our terror of the unknown."

French physiologist Claude Bernard said, "Man can learn nothing unless he proceeds from the known to the unknown."

And it was Defense Secretary Donald Rumsfeld who articulated, "There are known knowns. There are known unknowns; that is to say we know there are some things we do not know. But there are also unknown unknowns—the ones we don't know we don't know."

Perhaps it's Rumsfeld's insightful peeling back of the layers of truth in discovery that best describes how 99.9% of Americans consider the sport of curling. It's an unknown. We know it's an unknown. And even though its relation to shuffleboard—played exclusively by the over-seventy-five crowd or drunken college students in bars—is known, within curling's intricacies there are probably hundreds of unknown unknowns. But that's just a guess. We don't really know.

But what we do know, after consulting those in the know, is that curling is subject to many of the same injustices that befall our favorite mainstream American sports. And to hear Quebec coach Francois Roberge tell it, there is no greater curling calamity, or Canadian tragedy, than what happened to his team at the 2002 Brier.

The Brier, the annual Canadian men's curling championship, is like a multiple-team tournament version of our Super Bowl, minus the million-dollar commercials, one billion fans, and Janet Jackson's nipple. Winning the Brier is the pinnacle of any curler's "athletic" career. And thus, losing there because of a blown official's call is a catastrophe of the highest order.

In Quebec's opening match of the tournament's round-robin against Manitoba, an official moved one of Manitoba's rocks while trying to measure it. And because of that, and we apologize for using curling terms, it forced the teams to "replay the extra end," which allowed Manitoba to record "a last shot takeout" and ultimately win the match by one.

The stunned Quebecers complained, of course, prompting Brier officials to stop the "action" and confer on the decision for several minutes. But in the end it was decided that Manitoba's awarded replay was the appropriate remedy. The curling powers-that-be declared it a proper solution to an unfortunate incident.

A conclusion that didn't give the over-the-top Roberge one ounce of comfort.

"We were robbed, period," said the visibly shaken Roberge. "That was the worst call I've seen in my life. I don't know if someone can forget this. It's impossible. I'm going to have to live with it."

Perhaps, just maybe, Monsieur Markedly Emotional could use some perspective. Or at the very least a soporific prescription.

Ideally, the umpire should combine the integrity of a Supreme Court judge, the physical agility of an acrobat, the endurance of Job, and the imperturbability of Buddha.

—*Time Magazine*
AUGUST 25, 1961

Hey Earl, if you were my husband I'd feed you rat poison.

—HECKLING FEMALE FAN

If you were my wife, I'd eat it.

—EARL STROM
NBA AND ABA REFEREE (1957–1990)

Yes, honey . . . Just squeeze your rage up into a bitter little ball and release it at an appropriate time, like the day I hit the referee with the whiskey bottle.

—HOMER SIMPSON
AMERICAN PHILOSOPHER